Inca Civilization in Cuzco

INCA CIVILIZATION IN CUZCO

By R. Tom Zuidema

Translated from the French by
Jean-Jacques Decoster
Foreword by Françoise Héritier-Augé

University of Texas Press
Austin

La civilisation inca au Cuzco by R. Tom Zuidema
© Presses Universitaires de France, 1986
108, boulevard Saint-Germain, 75006 Paris

Translation and notes copyright © 1990 by the University of Texas Press
All rights reserved
Printed in the United States of America

First edition, 1990

Requests for permission to reproduce material from this work should
be sent to Permissions, University of Texas Press, Box 7819,
Austin, TX 78713-7819.

∞ The paper used in this publication meets the minimum requirements
of American National Standard for Information Sciences—
Permanence of Paper for Printed Library Materials, ANSI Z39.48-1984.

Library of Congress Cataloging-in-Publication Data

Zuidema, R. Tom (Reiner Tom), 1927–
  [Civilisation inca au Cuzco. English]
  Inca civilization in Cuzco / by R. Tom Zuidema ; translated by
Jean-Jacques Decoster ; foreword by Françoise Héritier-Augé. — 1st ed.
    p. cm.
  Translation of: La civilisation inca au Cuzco.
  Includes bibliographical references.
  ISBN 0-292-73850-1 (alk. paper). — ISBN 0-292-73851-X (pbk. : alk. paper)
  1. Incas—Social life and customs. 2. Incas—History. 3. Cuzco
(Peru)—Social life and customs. 4. Cuzco (Peru)—History. I. Title.
F3429.3.S6Z8213   1990
985′.37—dc20

                         89-77440
                            CIP

To Paquita, Annegien, and Lucho
with memories of the fieldtrips
we took together in the Andes

Contents

Figures

⊲ Foreword ⊳
TO THE FRENCH EDITION

I became acquainted with Professor R. Tom Zuidema as a result of his remarkable article "The Inca Kinship System: A New Theoretical View," which was a critical response to Floyd G. Lounsbury's formal analysis of that system in his paper "Some Aspects of the Inca Kinship System" (Lounsbury 1964). Working from sparse and not very explicit data, Lounsbury had reached conclusions of a sort to leave the reader puzzled and astonished at the Incas' ability to manipulate such a complex model: nothing less than the coexistence of parallel descent lines (agnatic for men, uterine for women) with two terminological systems, Omaha or Crow depending on whether the speakers are male or female. Zuidema's arguments demonstrated that this was not possible. He showed above all that there was no way to make any sense of the bits of information on kinship and marriage provided by the chroniclers until they were integrated into a much larger picture combining political and social organization and mythology with the calendar.

This work of synthesis Professor Zuidema undertook to present, at my invitation, in a series of lectures at the Collège de France in 1983–1984. The result is surprising and says a great deal about the capacity to manipulate reality of men who make the Inca sovereign's full sister into a "wife" who bears his only legitimate children, and his non-related wives into "sisters" who bear "nephews."

In fact this could only be a play on words. But from the ensuing classification of descent lines in relation to the patriline of the sovereign, there becomes evident the hierarchical principle that orders the administrators of the various districts into ranks marked by kinship terms situating them with regard to the Inca. Similarly, analysis of the myths—which supply the encompassing language of ideology and not, as the sixteenth-century Spaniards believed, the factual data of dynastic history—reveals a model for the political incorporation of conquered peoples carried out over three generations and ending by classifying the totality of the dependents in a relation of kinship to the sovereign.

In still more acute fashion, Zuidema shows us how the temporal organization of female age-classes (the Virgins of the Sun), in which women are recruited and classified according to their beauty, corresponds to a hierarchical structure developed on the same model as the organization of space. The organization of space is itself dependent on the *ceques,* a system of forty-one radiating lines that simultaneously divided space, according to precise astronomical observations, and the calendar. Associated in an unambiguous fashion with the districts, the *ceques* also permit the division of the year into an equal number of temporal sequences, which determine the ritual calendar and the terms of service to the King by the noble wives of the Incas-by-privilege—those "sisters" who give birth to "nephews." Zuidema shows us a rigorous mathematical structure, based on the observation of the heavens, which divides and governs time, space, ritual, and the lives of high-ranking women, priests, and everyone in the society; a structure that encompasses in a single explanatory principle genealogy and political space; a complete and admirably boundless structure that attempts to conjoin, rank, and explain everything, from the movement of the stars to the administration of the state, from the routine agricultural activities to the most problematic and undefinable thing in the world, beauty.

We thought we knew all about the Inca world. Thanks to this difficult book—for it is not simple to set forth and disentangle the interlaced threads of such a holistic system of representation—we can finally understand the peculiar genius of the Incas: an intellectual attempt to rationalize the world, allowing nothing at all to escape the grip of a single and unique interpretative grid.

Françoise Héritier-Augé
Professor at the Collège de France 1986

◄ Acknowledgments ►

During my first field trip to Peru, where I was investigating the forms of social organization characteristic of the Andean region, I took as a guide and constant inspiration Professor Claude Lévi-Strauss's then quite recent article "Do Dualistic Organizations Exist?", written in tribute to my teacher Professor J.-P.-B. de Josselin de Jong. Fieldwork carried out afterward in modern Andean communities and the analysis of Inca kinship and the details of the calendar prompted me to give further consideration to the questions propounded at that time, which are here developed in more depth. Thanks to the friendly efforts of Professor Pierre Duviols, the Ecole Pratique des Hautes Etudes procured me the opportunity to formulate my first conclusions on the Inca calendar. Professor Françoise Héritier-Augé's interest in Inca and Andean kinship led me to realize how fruitful such an analysis could be for anthropological theory in general. I am sincerely grateful to Professor Héritier-Augé and the Collège de France for their generous hospitality to my wife and me. These lectures were given in French, in December 1983 and January 1984. Tina Jolas reviewed them in preparation for the French publication thanks to a grant from the Research Board of the University of Illinois and that university's Center for Latin American and Caribbean Studies.

R.T.Z.

1986

Inca Civilization in Cuzco

1

Introduction

I would like to start with a consideration of some of the specific problems inherent in the study of Andean civilization as it was revealed to the Western world after the fall of the Inca state in 1532. At that time, much of the empire was torn by a civil war waged between the two brothers Atahuallpa and Huascar. The Spaniards, advancing in their conquest from Cajamarca in the north to the capital, Cuzco, in the south, came upon a number of provincial capitals, such as Vilcas Huaman, that had already been entirely deserted. When they arrived in Cuzco, they found that the victorious armies of Atahuallpa had plundered the city, stripping it of much of its gold and splendor, and putting to death most of the Inca nobility who had followed Huascar.

It is, however, only for Cuzco that Spanish chroniclers give the detailed—although somewhat idealized—information that allows us to study multiple aspects of Inca civilization: the spatial and temporal dimensions of social organization, kinship, age-classes, irrigation, architecture, art, the calendar, religion, and history. In fact, the wealth of written documents invites us to suggest a possible representation of Inca culture, and to attempt—at least for this one place in the Andes—a reconstruction that we hope to be as coherent and accurate as possible.[1]

This is not to say that the information we have for Cuzco is most abundant in all of those categories. On the contrary: the mythology of Huarochiri in central Peru, for example, is far better preserved, and seemingly in a purer and more indigenous form than that of Cuzco.[2] It is also true that the chroniclers writing in the capital tended to incorporate into myth narrative data of a different order, such as the interest that the Incas took in accounts of imperial expansion, or the desire the Spaniards had for the creation of a European-style dynasty. Nevertheless, only in Cuzco can one fully observe the process of integration of mythology into the global sociocultural organization. The same goes for art: that of some pre-Incaic cultures such as the Mochica or the coastal Nazca is better known and arguably more interesting to archaeologists, anthropologists, and art historians than the abstract geometrical art of the Incas, in spite of its remarkable technical qualities. But once again, only in Cuzco do we find the specific indications that allow us to place some of the artifacts in their precise mythical, ritual, architectural, and political context.

It is then understandable that Cuzco would occupy a privileged position in the historical and anthropological study of Andean culture at the time of the Conquest, in spite of the rich demographic as well as religious documentation that exists for other regions. And, unquestionably, such focus on Cuzco has through the centuries led to a dangerously distorted vision of Andean culture in general and of the Inca civilization in particular. A good example of that Cuzco-centered vision is the description of the city made by the Inca Garcilaso de la Vega in 1609, over seventy-five years after the Conquest, and it is often to that picture that Andean scholars refer when dealing with elements that are outside the range of their expertise.

Historians have not studied the Cuzco chronicles in order to elicit information on the specific local situation. Rather they have tended to use those texts to draw out elements of a broad representation of Andean culture. However, if we want to extend results obtained in Cuzco to other regions of Peru, we must first be able to compare them with detailed documents emanating from those same regions.

Thanks in part to my work on the calendar, I am now in a better position than before to present a study of Cuzco in a regional perspective: a city surrounded, in a radius of some fifty kilometers, by various groups of non-Inca origin with which it had social, matrimonial, and economic relations. Those groups, known as Incas-by-privilege, had to be periodically represented at the court of the Inca king, and in turn were granted land in the valley to provide for their needs.

I will introduce my description of the social system in the Cuzco Valley with a new analysis of the Inca myth of origin, a myth that specifically refers to the relation between Incas and Incas-by-privilege, and that alludes more or less directly to all the themes that I propose to consider later on.[3] But before examining the myth, let me reflect on some methodological issues that have directed this approach.

Theoretical developments of the past forty years have led to notable methodological improvements. Leaving Cuzco outside the scope of his investigations, John Murra concentrated his research on the economic and social conditions in Inca provinces such as Huánuco and Chucuito, basing his study on the extensive documentation provided by the "Visitas" that took place some thirty years after the Conquest.[4] Pierre Duviols offered an exhaustive historiographic critique of the chroniclers and focused the studies on the sixteenth- and seventeenth-century documents dealing with the "Extirpation of Idolatries" (Duviols 1971; 1986). Maria Rostworowski (1988) and Waldemar Espinoza in numerous publications in Peru and Nathan Wachtel (1971; 1973) in France advanced notably the historiography of Inca society and its aftermath in early colonial times.

In all of those studies, with the exception, perhaps, of the mythology of Huarochiri, written in Quechua, we are confronted with an obvious problem: the fact that all the sources are in Spanish, and that they are accompanied by interpretations, also mostly given by the Spaniards. Unfortunately, we do not have for the Andes sources comparable to the prehispanic Mesoamerican codices such as the Dresden Codex, which would allow us a systematic control of our interpretations as well of those of the chroniclers.

My purpose is to subject the study of Andean civilization to more critical forms of investigation, and I have chosen to emphasize three methodological approaches. First, I have taken as the object of my analysis descriptions by the chroniclers of systems remarkable for their level of complexity, and I will argue that such structural complexity in itself attests a prehispanic origin. In fact, very few systems of this type exist. One of them is the organization of space by way of the *ceque* system: the forty-one directions radiating from the Temple of the Sun in Cuzco that organized the 328 topographical sites or *huacas*—a system that always has been an important point of reference in my research. It is the relation between the *ceque* system and the Inca calendar that here suggests a prehispanic origin. Another way to ascertain the purely indigenous character of a theme is to compare it to cultural traits observable in other, non-Andean South American Indian societies that, until recent years, had been spared the structural changes occasioned by Western influence. I will in that respect mention the Inca system of age-classes, whose complex structure is strikingly similar to those found among Gê tribes of Eastern Brazil.

Another methodological approach that helps us to understand facts rooted in the prehispanic past involves on-site verification of all the names cited in myths, rituals, social organization, irrigation systems, and astronomical data. This method, which also benefits from archaeological research, has been extremely productive in my recent investigations in Cuzco. I consider it to be at the moment the best support in solving the theoretical problems that I propose.

A third method, which I will have to leave aside for the time being, takes into consideration Inca art in the specific instances where a description by the chroniclers corresponds point by point to the iconographic structure of a prehispanic artifact.

In all of these approaches, I start from reliable Spanish sources and attempt to isolate themes capable of contributing to anthropological theory. I do not claim to construct an explanatory sketch of Inca culture, but only to bring together materials that will allow us to redefine our interpretations as the research progresses. Having one case available in the Andes, that of Cuzco, which allows us to analyze and solve problems of complex structures on the basis of written documentation, we may expect to find similar types of problems elsewhere.

The central theme of my reflection will be the kinship model considered—and reformulated, where necessary—in terms of the organization of space in the Cuzco Valley, of the irrigation system, of the administrative structure, of the age-class system, and, finally, of the calendar and calendric rituals and myths.

Let me define and limit somehow the questions that I intend to address. Following the publication of my book on Cuzco (Zuidema 1964), I focused my research on two problems related to the Inca empire: kinship nomenclature (Zuidema 1977a; 1989a) and, later, Inca astronomy considered in relation to the state calendar and to all the spatio-temporal aspects of political organization (1977b and later). First I had attempted to explain the kinship terminology, concentrating on the interpretation of one element, namely the equivalence between mother's brother and wife's father, suggested by the Quechua term *caca* applied indifferently to either of these relatives. This equivalence seemed to me to indicate that we were dealing with a marriage system known as "generalized exchange" or "asymmetrical alliance." My fieldwork on contemporary Andean culture later led me to conclude that such a system, in which one marries a real or classificatory mother's brother's daughter, does not exist and never existed in the Andes. One does not marry a first cousin, and furthermore, there is a marked preference for symmetrical rather than asymmetrical exchanges. Within the limits of my article on kinship, I was unable to apply my new interpretations to the whole of the sociopolitical and hierarchical organization of Cuzco. This is what I intend to do in the two following chapters dealing with spatial organization.

The analysis of the calendar will allow us to study the system of calendrical rites and the corresponding myths, and more generally the whole temporal organization of Cuzco. The Inca calendar was a very delicate and highly precise system whose code I believe I have finally broken. To a division of the Inca society into twelve groups corresponded a calendrical division of twelve months. Each of those twelve groups was responsible for the celebration of rituals in a given month.[5] In addition, the organization of time according to the calendrical constraints directed the organization of the provinces around the Cuzco Valley. It also played a determining role in marriage structures as well as in political and economic alliances in which the number 40 assumed an exceptional importance.

During the academic year 1982–1983, the Ecole Pratique des

Figure 1. Map of the Cuzco region. By Colin McEwan.

Hautes Etudes in Paris gave me the opportunity to present a first reconstruction of the Inca calendar. In the present work, I intend to develop in more depth the question of time (Chapters 4 and 5). With that purpose in mind, I will first consider the problem of age-classes, and more specifically its female aspect, given the mediating position of the organization of age-classes in relation to that of royal ancestors, on the one hand, and of the calendrical rites, on the other. Then, situating the notion of "time" in a broader context, I will study the whole political organization of Cuzco in its temporal aspect. Finally, I will consider the problem of marriage alliances between Inca lords and non-Incas, always in relation to the calendar, which, here again, plays a crucial role.

Some practical information about Cuzco might be useful at this point. The city is situated in southern Peru, at a latitude of 13.5 degrees south and an altitude of over 3,200 meters. The Cuzco Valley, 20 kilometers long from west to east, comprises the upper course of the Huatanay River which feeds into the Villcanota River, or the Urubamba, as it is also called in its middle part. Only one chronicler, writing in the first years after the Conquest (Molina "el Almagrista" p. 67; Cook pp. 211–219; Rowe 1967 p. 60 and n. 14), gives us an estimate of the population of Cuzco: over 40,000 families for the city and 200,000 families for the region within the 50–60-kilometer radius where the Incas-by-privilege lived. However, I put little faith in that estimate: 40,000 was the figure used by the Inca state to indicate the administrative ranking of an imperial province (Santillán; Guaman Poma; Murúa; Cobo Bk. 12, Ch. 25), and therefore that figure should not be taken as an indication of the actual total population. We will have to resort to other methods to estimate the population density in the city of Cuzco and its province, that is to say, to arrive at a census that would include the Incas-by-privilege.[6] Nonetheless, the figure of 40,000 will prove to be very useful in my study of marriage alliances between Inca and non-Inca lords.

The Origin Myth

Let me introduce a description of the organization of Cuzco, its valley, and its province by way of its myth of origin, which gives us a global vision of the political situation at the time of first European contact. I examine three versions of the myth in order to extract the specific details they provide about problems of kinship, age-classes, and the concepts of spatial organization. As my argument is guided by a progressive logic, I consider first a rather late version; but one that originates in the works of an indigenous author (Fig. 2).

Juan de Santacruz Pachacuti Yamqui (pp. 284–287) tells us how Manco Capac, the founding ancestor of the Inca dynasty, reached

Figure 2. The house of Manco Capac, by Santacruz Pachacuti. From *Relación de antigüedades deste reyno del Pirú* by Joan de Santacruz Pachacuti Yamqui Salcamaygua.

Cuzco from Lake Titicaca. At the time of his arrival, the region was split into two kingdoms: that of King Tocay Capac, north of Cuzco, and that of King Pinahua Capac in the south. Interestingly, those two kingdoms, seen as a projection of the city toward the outside, correspond to the division of Cuzco into two moieties, Hanan Cuzco or "Upper Cuzco" and Hurin Cuzco or "Lower Cuzco" (Zuidema 1977a pp. 274–275).

To confirm his conquest and appropriation of the two kingdoms, and to mark his accession to the throne, Manco Capac had the houses of the two previous kings destroyed and a new one built for himself. The genealogical model constructed by Santacruz Pachacuti also takes the shape of a house. His drawing shows one with three windows (Fig. 2). A golden tree connects the central window, where Manco Capac's first ascending generation of ancestors is represented, to the right window occupied by his paternal ancestors. In the same way, a silver tree connects the central window to the left window where his maternal ancestors are represented. His father is called "Lord House," and "house" is also the name of the central window. His mother is called "Earth-Mother-Diviner." The two trees are, in the same manner labeled *tampo*, "house," for the golden tree, and *huaca*, "sacred place," for the silver one. Thus we can see Manco Capac as the ancestor of the royal dynasty, born of the union between the human occupation of the land and the land itself. The capitals of the two conquered kingdoms, Maras and Sutic, lend their names to the two lateral windows, from which we can infer that conquered enemies are adopted as ancestors.[7]

According to other versions of the myth, the windows of Manco Capac's house were the openings of a cave, Tambotoco, which can still be found near the village of Pacaritambo, about 30 kilometers south of Cuzco (Fig. 1). Manco Capac came out of the cave with three brothers and four sisters. The oldest version of the myth, that of Juan de Betanzos (1987 Part 1, Chs. 3–5), is particularly interesting with regard to this episode. It mentions four couples, each consisting of one brother and his spouse, emerging from the cave one after the other. Together, they set out toward Cuzco, but on the way three of the brothers turn into stone. Manco Capac is the only brother to reach the city, and here he builds the Temple of the Sun, which will become the house of his four sisters. The first brother to emerge from the cave is Ayar Cachi, "Ancestor Salt." He is prodigiously strong. When the four couples see Cuzco for the first time from the top of Mount Huanacauri, at the southeastern side of the valley, Ayar Cachi picks up his sling and throws stones into the four directions, creating the mountains and valleys of the Inca land and giving it the shape that can still be seen today. The brothers of Ayar Cachi send him back to the cave they all came from, where he turns into stone, and there he remains the object of a cult as the subterranean ancestor of the Incas.

The second brother, Ayar Uchu, "Ancestor *Capsicum* Pepper," turns into stone on top of Mount Huanacauri, and he will be the ancestor of the priests (Sarmiento Ch. 12). The third brother, Ayar Auca, "Ancestor Warrior," is transformed into stone in Cuzco itself, and he is known as the "owner of the land" (Sarmiento Ch. 13). Manco Capac himself will also eventually turn into stone, but as the ancestor of the royal dynasty.

Four different roles are thus attributed to the four brothers. But we also see that the succession of transformations into stone follows a spatial progression. The last two brothers are identified with Cuzco itself, either as king or as owner/conqueror of the territory where the capital is erected. As for the first two brothers, they are associated with the outskirts of the valley, that is to say, with the land occupied by the Incas-by-privilege. The first Ayar turns into stone on that territory itself, and the second at the boundary between non-Inca territory and the Inca valley. This part of the origin myth contains another remarkable episode, the birth of the son of Manco Capac, which took place *before* the group of travelers reached Huanacauri, and the initiation rites for the child, performed *after* they had left Huanacauri for the Cuzco Valley (Sarmiento Ch. 12).

Finally, in 1572, Pedro Sarmiento de Gamboa (pp. 116–135) added to the first two themes of the myth—the three windows and the four couples—a third one: Sarmiento's version says that ten groups of people also emerge from Tambotoco and accompany Manco Capac and his brothers and sisters to Cuzco. The five groups belonging to Hanan Cuzco (Upper Cuzco) come out of Maras Toco, the right-hand window; the other five groups, of Hurin Cuzco (Lower Cuzco),

Hanan-Cuzco

Chinchaysuyu (I) (northwest)	Chavin Cuzco Arayraca Cuzco Callan Huacaytaqui	Tarpuntay Sañu (Yacanora, Ayarmaca, Cari)	Antisuyu (III) (northeast)

Hurin-Cuzco

Cuntisuyu (IV) (southwest)	Masca Oro (Anahuarque)	Sutic Maras Cuicusa	Collasuyu (II) (southeast)

Figure 3. The non- or pre-Inca *ayllus* of Cuzco. (I have added some names, indicated in parentheses, to the ten groups that came to Cuzco from the outside. The additional groups belong to the pre-Inca or autocthonous population of the valley; I will come to them later.)

emerge from the left-hand window, Sutic Toco. The names of the groups are extremely interesting because they reveal the characteristics of their spatial distribution over the two moieties and the four subdivisions (or *suyus*) of the territory whose boundaries were set by Ayar Cachi and his sling (Fig. 3).

Other sources attest to the pre- or non-Inca origin of the ten groups (Zuidema 1964 pp. 192–199). Two of them, Chavin Cuzco Ayllu and Arayraca Ayllu Cuzco Callan, arrived in Cuzco before the Incas did. In spite of their pre-Incaic origin, the two groups claimed as their ancestors Ayar Uchu and Ayar Cachi, the first two of Manco Capac's brothers who emerged with him from the cave. Those two groups belonged to the first *suyu* (Suyu I) of Hanan Cuzco. Two other groups, Maras and Sutic, bore the same names as the capitals of the pre-Incaic kingdoms that were identified with the two moieties in their provincial extensions. It is, however, interesting to note that their representation at the Inca court did not reflect that division in the same way. There, Maras and Sutic were both members of Suyu II, the most important *suyu* in Hurin Cuzco. While they were diametrically opposed to each other at the level of the two provincial moieties of Hanan and Hurin, Maras and Sutic shared a common concentric opposition in relation to Cuzco. In their position at the court, this opposition of the periphery to the center was expressed by another opposition, this time diametrical, between the groups connected to Manco Capac and the Ayar brothers on the one hand, and, on the other, the representatives of Maras and Sutic, the two pre-Incaic capitals.

The groups that made up Suyus III and IV raise similar problems. Sañu, a village located in the center of the valley and belonging to Suyu III, was a regional capital when Manco Capac arrived. Masca is the name of the territory occupied by Incas-by-privilege to the south of Cuzco where Tambotoco and Pacaritambo are located. This last group is represented at the court by Suyu IV of Hurin Cuzco. Again we have a different example of an initial concentric opposition between two villages which is translated into a diametrical opposition in the way those populations are represented at the court.

In addition to those problems of concentric and diametrical opposition that refer to concepts of spatial organization, there is a problem of a different order that the names of two other groups in Hanan Cuzco allow us to apprehend more clearly. Tarpuntay does not refer to a local origin, but rather indicates a class of priests. The word *tarpuntay* derives from *tarpuy*, "to plant." Those priests performed extremely important functions at the time of planting and at other times of the agricultural cycle (Molina "el Cuzqueño" 1943 pp. 26, 28, 50, 54, 67, 81; Cobo Bk. 13, Chs. 25, 28). The Tarpuntay were also considered as priests of the Sun (Cobo Bk. 13, Ch. 33). Their sacerdotal function was not necessarily hereditary: individual calling, social rank, membership in a specific age-class, and birth order within a family all played a possible role in the constitution of the group as priests. It seems that similar considerations were involved in the establishment of the group or class of Huacaytaqui, the "Singers and Dancers of the Shrines," and that such considerations might also have played a part in the formation of all other groups in spite of their territorial names.

The problems raised by the myth of origin, problems that all deal with the organization of pre-Incaic peoples in the valley and the province of Cuzco, anticipate the ones that we will have to consider in relation to the dominating and governing class of the Incas themselves. The divisions indicated by the names of the windows of Tambotoco and by those of Manco Capac's brothers and sisters refer us back to the question of the ten non-Inca groups involved in the organization of Cuzco itself. How are we to interpret the fact that they were represented at the court, in Cuzco, or even in the valley? We know that Sañu, Chavin Cuzco, and Arayraca Cuzco were autochthonous groups present in the valley well before the arrival of the Incas. But in the cases of Maras, Sutic, and Masca, I think that those are political groups that always lived outside of Cuzco, but who could be represented there at certain times of the year, and by certain individuals specially designated. According to one of our oldest sources (Santo Thomás pp. 128–129), Maras and Sutic were families that used to provide servants to the Inca nobility. The myth of origin analyzes the relations between groups in terms of kinship, age-classes, profession, and territory. This information, contained in the myth itself, is often so mingled that it is difficult to separate the different kinds of data. It seems, however, that the purpose of the myth is precisely to synthesize all this information, and it might be preferable, for the time being, not to try to sort it out.

As an example of this type of problem, I will conclude with a reference to the word *tambo*, which we have already met as the designation of the central window of Tambotoco (Zuidema 1964 pp. 86–88). The Tambos were a group of Incas-by-privilege of a higher rank than the rest, a group assimilated to Inca nobles who had torn earlobes, and we know that pierced earlobes with large earplugs were a characteristic sign of nobility. These Tambo nobles occupied administrative positions similar to those of Inca nobles. This is why, even knowing the name and other specifics concerning a dignitary in such position, we can never be certain whether he was truly of royal blood or from the noble Tambo caste, or whether he had been born of a marriage between the two groups, or had been granted that rank on other personal grounds. Thus, before taking into account specific individual cases, it is the whole system of the ten groups that we must attempt to understand, and to understand precisely as a system.

◄ 2 ►

The Administration of the *Chapa* Districts in the Cuzco Valley

The origin myth gave us a first global vision of the Inca organization in Cuzco and the whole province, including the territories of the Incas-by-privilege. The myth is a simplification of a much more complex situation, as it takes into account only ten groups, of which only a few lived permanently in the valley. We must note, however, that all of these groups were politically represented at the Court. I would like to examine what can be inferred from the corpus of ethno-historical and ethnological data regarding this territorial division of the valley.

Let us first consider one piece of information found in the descriptions that the first chronicler of Cuzco, Betanzos (1987 Part 1, Chs. 12, 13, 16, pp. 55–63, 75–79; Zuidema in press a; in press b), gives us concerning the administrative reorganization of the valley conducted by royal decree. We cannot attribute a historical or chronological value to this information, and, for the time being, the name of the king is irrelevant.

In his enterprise of reorganization, the king was assisted by ten Inca lords and twenty nobles. We can assume that each lord was assisted by two nobles. They all had to find, in the villages of the Incas-by-privilege, food for the workers involved in the execution of the public works. One of the tasks consisted of the canalization, over a distance of 20 kilometers, of the riverbed throughout the valley. Each lord was in charge of the canalization of a portion of the river—a method of division of labor still in use in modern villages—and of the construction and maintenance of the irrigation channels. Moreover, the king made grants to his vassals of land located on the mountainside and corresponding to sections of the river. Each lord of the Incas-by-privilege was allowed to build storehouses in the section or district to which he was assigned, called a *chapa*, for the products that he brought from his villages.

It is on the basis of these organizational modalities that I will identify a system of Inca administration in the Cuzco Valley: the ten *chapas* as ruled by ten relatives of the Inca king. In order to facilitate the argument, I have located the *chapas*, approximately and within the two moieties and the four *suyus*, on the map of the valley (Fig. 4).[8] As territorial units involved in the distribution of water, the *chapa* districts were independent from one another. But they were hierarchically ranked, taking into account two considerations: the Hanan districts, served by wider irrigation networks, were superior to those of Hurin; and in general the upriver districts were superior to the downriver ones. For Cuntisuyu (IV), which was lower in rank in Hurin-Cuzco than Collasuyu (II) but upriver, other considerations of ranking were taken into account (Zuidema 1964; 1986; Villanueva and Sherbondy 1984 p. 53).

There were thus ten districts administered by the king assisted by members of the Inca nobility. These ten Inca lords were seconded by non-Inca lords and nobles who benefited from certain territorial rights within the valley, which in turn guaranteed their representation at the Court. These rights concerned the same ten districts, which I have numbered from 10 to 1, in descending hierarchical order. The king formed with the non-Inca lords treaties that could lead to marriage alliances.[9]

I will analyze first the role of the royal relatives in the administration of the *chapas*, and then move on to the question of marriage alliances. The rank order of these relatives was conditioned by that of the *chapas* that they governed, and each rank was expressed by a kin term that situated the individual in relation to the king. This fact will allow us to narrow down the concept of *ayllu*, a term that connotes a political and social unit, as well as a kin group, or even the very no-

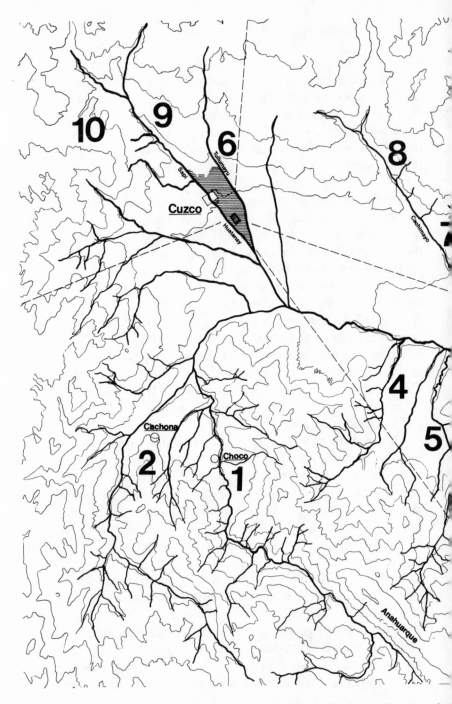

Figure 4. The ten *chapas* of the Cuzco Valley. Drawn by Kevin Rotheroe. The approxim
location of the ten *chapas* in the river and irrigation system of the Cuzco Valley is indica
by the numbers of the *panacas*. Sañu, Oma, Choco, and Cachona are autocthonous villa

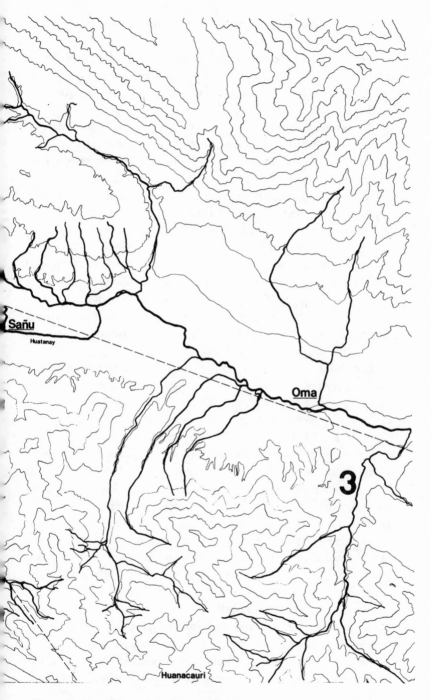

The *ayllus* Yacanora, Ayarmaca, and Cari (Fig. 3) are located in the Sañu and Oma region and are mentioned for the *ceques* of III-3 (see Figs. 16 and 17). Anahuarque is the sacred mountain of Choco and Cachona.

tion of "kin."[10] I have already, in my article on the Inca kinship system, studied the kinship terminology and the general concept of *ayllu;* however, I was not able then to fully appreciate the relevance of this concept for the hierarchical organization of the royal family.

But before dealing with the notion of Inca hierarchy from the perspective of kinship, I would like to further comment on a point related to the *chapas,* being involved in the distribution of water for irrigation. There was in Peru (Avila Ch. 31; Zuidema 1985b pp. 48–51; 1986 [1978])—and still is in specific traditional contexts (Arguedas 1956)—an important distinction between the ownership of the irrigation water, the usufruct of it, and the administrative grouping by which several *ayllus* or water districts formed a single homogenous political unit. We know that in various parts of the Andes irrigation water was the property of the original settlers, who formed the lower social strata. People of a higher rank could obtain rights over the water only with the consent of the small farmers, first users of the irrigation water. Myths (which I will relate further on) lead us to believe that the situation was similar in Cuzco.

The chronicles that mention the administrative system operating in the valley refer to two traditions. The most ancient, and the one closest to the origin myth, comes from two chroniclers: Bartolomé de las Casas (Vol. 4, Ch. 251, p. 398) and Pedro Gutiérrez de Santa Clara (Vol. 3, Ch. 50, p. 214).[11] The former had never set foot in Peru, and possibly neither had the latter (Bataillon 1961). I will demonstrate, however, that this tradition emanates from an author who knew perfectly well the local conditions in Cuzco. As for the second tradition, that of the indigenous chronicler writing at a later date, Felipe Guaman Poma de Ayala (pp. 288[290], 738–740 [752–754]), it offers a very complex image of the whole Inca administrative system; but, curiously enough, Guaman Poma is also the only important chronicler who does not mention the territorial divisions of the Cuzco Valley.

Las Casas and Gutiérrez tell us, each in his own way, that the organizer-king (for Gutiérrez, he is the actual conqueror of Cuzco) divided the valley into ten sections—in which we recognize the ten *chapas*—and gave the administration of each section to a kinsman of his. He proceeded in the following manner: he reserved for himself the administration of the second of the five sections in Hanan-Cuzco and assigned the administration of the third, fourth, and fifth to individuals who were related to him respectively through his father, his grandfather, and his great-grandfather. The administration of the first section, which was called Capac Ayllu, the "Royal Group," was given to his son. In Hurin-Cuzco, he distributed the sections in the same fashion among people related to him through so-called "secondary" brothers of the individuals mentioned above. We can already make one preliminary observation: in each moiety, the organizer-king gives the administration of four sections to relatives of his own age-group and one to a relative, namely his son, of a different age-group. He himself assumes the role of mediator: he articulates between the two types of distribution, the one horizontal and the other vertical. We also notice in this myth that the redistribution is effected *before* the organizer is crowned king. Hence the possibility for us to see here a model comparable to the one outlined in the myth of Manco Capac and his brothers. In that myth the birth and initiation of Manco Capac's son occur along the way—respectively before and after the passing of Mount Huanacauri—and his coronation as first king of Cuzco takes place only *after* the conquest of Cuzco. The organizer-king that I evoke here had repelled an attack on Cuzco when he was still only heir to the crown. I analyze elsewhere this story in which I see the myth underlying the initiation rites of young men and women of the Inca nobility (Zuidema 1985a). The administrative organization of the Cuzco Valley appears then as an act of reorganization and restatement of the power structure, accomplished by each successive king at the time of his accession to the throne.

Although the second tradition—that told by Guaman Poma de Ayala—deals with the same model, it is not there represented by an ascending patriline and nine other, cognatic, lines, but rather by a single descending line originating with the king himself. Guaman Poma mentions this mode of representation on two separate occasions. The first time is when he relates the election of a new king. At the death of the old king, he explains, all his sons, legitimate and illegitimate, and all the lords Capac Apu of the kingdom had to do penance and fast. Then the legitimate sons, of whom there "could be one, two, three, or four," would offer sacrifices in the Temple of the Sun. The Sun would pick a king among them, and the chosen one could very well be the youngest son. At this point all the courtiers changed genealogical positions vis-à-vis the dead king and acquired new positions vis-à-vis the reigning monarch. From then on, the legitimate kin were said to be *auquicuna,* or "royal princes," the illegitimate kin to be the "nephews and nieces," and the Capac Apu to be the "grandchildren."

Returning later to the same question, Guaman Poma refines the model. He now establishes subdivisions within the *auquicuna* group, who, jointly, are called *capac churi,* "royal sons"; he distinguishes among them between "sons," "grandsons," "great-grandsons," and "great-great-grandsons," according to a descending hierarchical order. However, he puts the great-great-grandsons on the same horizontal genealogical level as the nephews, assigning these two groups of descendants to the two moieties of Hanan- and Hurin-Cuzco, respectively (Fig. 5). But all these relatives were also considered, re-

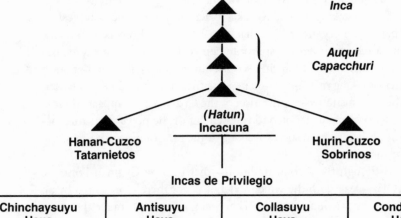

Figure 5. The Inca genealogical ranks according to Guaman Poma de Ayala. (*Tatarnietos* = great-great-grandsons; *sobrinos* = nephews; Incas de Privilegio = Incas-by-privilege.)

spectively, as "sons" and "nephews" of the king, so that the "great lords," or Capac Apu, belonging to the four *suyus* or provinces of the empire, were once again considered as "grandsons." We conclude that in the two examples we are dealing with one and the same organization, made up of either three or six genealogical levels; and we note that a relative considered as, say, "grandson of the king" could at the same time be recognized—according to the Las Casas and Gutiérrez model—as classificatory "brother" or "cousin," related to the king through a common grandfather. What matters is the genealogical distance to the king himself or to the common ancestor. Guaman Poma discusses here a hierarchical system of genealogical titles and ranks, and not of actual genealogical positions and relations in a descending line. The king was a reigning king, who during his life never could possibly have true great-great-great-grandsons. It is indeed a very complex system, in many ways comparable to the one that prevailed at the court of Louis XIV, another Sun-King, as it has been described by the Princess Palatine and the Duke of Saint-Simon (Héritier 1981 p. 52; Le Roy Ladurie 1973).

From a comparison of the two models—the one ascending and the other descending—we can draw the elements of a unified model and study its characteristics and structure. The central problem lies in the use, noted by Guaman Poma, of the term *concha*, "nephew," a term which in the colonial society served to designate free but landless peasants. Betanzos indicates that in Inca society the term *concha*, that is "child of a man's sister," was used by the Inca king under the form of *huaccha concha*, "poor nephew" or "orphan nephew," to refer to his *own* children by non-Inca women; that is women belonging to the class of Incas-by-privilege, themselves referred to as *huaccha* (or *uaccha*), "poor" (Fig. 5). Furthermore, Betanzos also indicates, and so does Guaman Poma, that the *huaccha concha* belonged to the lower moiety (i.e., Hurin-Cuzco). For reasons that I will soon explain, I argue that if the king distinguished between two of his sons—one being *churi*, "son," and the other *concha*, "sister's son"—it was in order to arrange the group of these sons in so many "pairs" and to establish hierarchical distinctions between the individuals thus paired. The use of this type of distinction helps us to understand the reason for the existence not only of the Hanan and Hurin

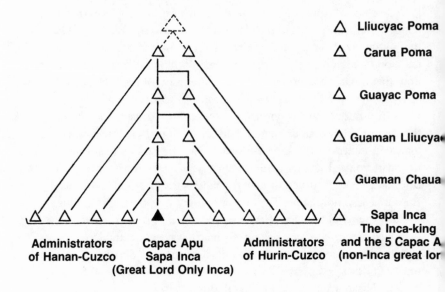

Figure 6. The royal family (Capac Ayllu) in Cuzco.

moieties, but also of the internal divisions within the two moieties (Fig. 6).

The central line, the king's patriline, was called *checan ceque,* "straight line," and the nine cognatic lines, *pallcarec ceque,* from *pallca,* "bifurcation," and also "tree branch" or "river arm" (Pérez Bocanegra). Those were lines that each originated from a secondary son called "sister's son"—lineages, then, to which this name conferred a matrilineal kind of value, without their having to be matrilines in a strict genealogical sense. But if the term *huaccha concha,* "poor nephews," designates the group of royal secondary sons, children of non-Inca, non-related women, there should then be social classifications within the group of Inca nobles, by which the lines issuing from the king—i.e., the straight line and the four branched lines—represented so many distinct hierarchical values, regulated by different marriage rules. In fact, we can study the administrative model of the royal family as the most explicit expression of the hierarchical Andean concept of the *ayllu.*

The Kin Model of the Royal Ayllu

The kin model that I attempt to construct is based on the myth of a man destined to be king. But I propose to look at it as a general model, equally valid for the administrative organization of the Inca society. For that reason, I would like to analyze this model in relation to my articles on Inca kinship (Zuidema 1977a; 1989a).[12]

As I intend to stress the hierarchical character of the system, I need first to answer the following question: if the children of marriages with non-Inca women are all classified as belonging to Hurin-Cuzco, why are there here too, according to the model of Las Casas and Gutiérrez, five hierarchical levels? Guaman Poma (pp. 75–76) gives us an answer in speaking about himself and his own family. According to him, his great-grandfather was originally an independent king in central Peru, a Capac Apu, just like the Inca king. For the moment it matters little whether Guaman Poma is relating an authentic historical fact or is using a "tactic" aimed at drawing the attention of the king of Spain to his chronicle by addressing him, in his "Letter to the King," as an equal. What interests us is the model that he uses. Later, the ancestor of Guaman Poma supposedly made a pact with the Inca king, and was hence recognized as governor of a vast Inca province, the size of which is indicated by the figure of forty thousand families, comparable in importance to the province of Cuzco itself. The Inca king gave his younger legitimate daughter in marriage to Guaman Poma's grandfather, who had inherited the rank of Capac Apu, Great Lord. As seen from his grandfather's position, Guaman Poma describes a hierarchical system consisting of five administrative titles of lords Capac Apu, titles that I have included in Figure 6, alongside the Inca hierarchical model. There are two Guaman ("Falcon") titles and three Poma ("Puma") ones. The names Chaua and Carua both have connotations related to dryness. Lliucyac means "Thunder," more precisely the thunder associated with rainstorms. One Guaman title is missing: the one corresponding to Guayac Poma, "Ferocious Puma." Undoubtedly, the Inca king occupied in this model the first place in a six-rank order. In any case, the hierarchical ranks could also find their expression in kinship terms (Zuidema 1983). For instance, the function of Lliucyac Poma could be filled by the son or grandson of a Guaman Chaua. And Guaman Poma (p. 435 [455]) explains his own name this way: Guaman because his grandfather was a Guaman Chaua, and Poma because his father was a younger son, i.e., a *concha* or "nephew." At this point, what interests us is the possibility of explaining the five hierarchical ranks found in Hurin-Cuzco as so many genealogical ranks implying marriages between Incas and ranked non-Inca women.

But let us return to the ten genealogical ranks found in Hanan- and Hurin-Cuzco. I will base my explanation of this system on three types of information: (1) the exclusive right the king had to marry his sister by the same father and same mother; (2) the distinction that he could make in kin terms between a "son" and a "sister's son," a distinction that applied to each "pair" of male descendants; and (3) the fact that the whole non-Inca and pre-Inca population of the valley was recognized as *cacacuzco*, i.e., "the affinal relatives of a man residing in the Cuzco valley" (Rostworowski 1962).

When I was studying the Quechua-Inca marriage system and kinship terminology (Zuidema 1977a), I found the graphic representation of the Inca genealogical system by the chronicler, Juan Pérez Bocanegra (1631) very useful (Fig. 7). In his drawing, the male line is called "straight line"; women in the female line are classified as daughters: *pihui ususi* is "older daughter, first daughter, principal daughter," and the great-great-granddaughter is called *sullca usus*, "younger or youngest daughter." I had used the model to account for the general rule that governs marriage in Inca society—a rule that to this day is still implicitly recognized—according to which relatives may contract marriage only at the generation of great-great-grandchildren. I had already written my article when I became aware,[13] that the model as it is represented (but without the Inca portraits that Pérez Bocanegra uses to illustrate each generation, and without the kinship terms) was of European origin. Pérez Bocanegra had quite judiciously selected his model to account for an Andean reality. Nevertheless, I plan to demonstrate that there existed Andean prehispanic models very similar to the one that he presented. To this end, I will analyze two examples.

The first example is from the Aymara language and is found in Ludovico Bertonio's dictionary (1612) with the following glosses:

Figure 7. The genealogical model of Pérez Bocanegra. (After Pedro come, over four generations, one line of sons and one line of daughters.) From J. Pérez Bocanegra, *Ritual formulario*, 1631.

Lari means "male relative of a woman," and, adds Bertonio, "this term is used also by that woman's son to designate those same male relatives of his mother." The redoubling of the word, *lari lari*, defines its territorial context: it applies to the surroundings of a town or a village where the non-kin, the uncivilized, the lawless people live. In the same context, Bertonio also gives the term *quimsacallco lari* for all the wife's relatives. The literal meaning of the term is "the eight *lari*." What then are those eight categories of *lari*? I believe that the term is better understood as the designation for the group of eight possible lines—one agnatic line and seven cognatic ones—which constitute a man's descent over four generations (Fig. 8).

This model not only fits within the semantic field defined by the word *lari lari,* but also covers the genealogical field determined by Pérez Bocanegra's model. Furthermore, the Aymara version gives us some information on specific consequences of marriage rules, of which I was not aware, and to which my attention was drawn by the works of John Earls (1971) on modern Andean kinship, and those of Françoise Héritier (1981) on the African Samo system as compared to the Andean system. In the first place, the information that we have from Bertonio stresses the fact that for five generations the wife and her family are outside the husband's family. In addition, the positive marriage rules on which I had based my argument authorized the

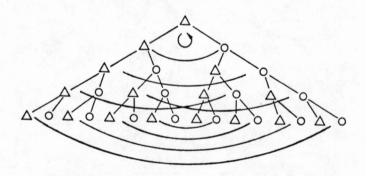

Figure 8. The eight (classes of) male relatives of the wife and the five hierarchical marriage possibilities (suggested by the kinship taxonomy given by Ludovico Bertonio in his Aymara dictionary).

marriage between relatives connected by one common great-great-grandfather, and admitted one form of preferential marriage: the symmetrical marriage between second-degree cross-cousins. My mistake was to postulate the equivalence of these two types of rules, as if they expressed the same reality, which is not true. The third-generation relatives are already second-degree cross-cousins, whereas those of the fourth generation are third-degree cross-cousins. We cannot posit an equivalence between those two types of rules, and what indeed needs to be defined is the relation between them.

I will attempt now to analyze the hierarchical organization of the different marriage rules, all of them symmetric in nature, which gravitate between two poles: that of the marriage of the king with his sister, the ultimate case of endogamy, and that of his marriage with a non-kin, here the ultimate case of exogamy. We know that the high nobility were allowed to marry among first-degree cross-cousins. Thus we can postulate the rule that individuals of the same genealogical rank in relation to the king could intermarry in order to guarantee the transmission of their own rank to their descendants. I have described in Figure 8 the hierarchical marriage possibilities using curved lines that link pairs of brothers and sisters. The possible symmetrical exchanges at each genealogical level are represented by one single line. The marriage of the king with his sister, corresponding to the first generation, is indicated by a circular arrow closing on itself. The high nobility, who marry among half-siblings and parallel cousins, are represented by the second generation, and the nobility who marry among cross-cousins, by the third generation. One chronicler explains how, in practice, this type of rule was applied. Pedro Pizarro (pp. 53–54), one of the very few Spaniards who had the opportunity to observe Inca life in Cuzco in the first year after the Conquest when it was still almost entirely intact, relates how he once had to assume the function of "marriage broker" for an Inca noble. The woman sought served in the temple of her own royal ancestor's mummy. When the mummy was asked for its authorization to the marriage, it answered through the intermediary of a man and a woman officiating at the temple: in their capacity as priests of the mummy, they were the ones who judged the compatibility between the future spouses.

We have observed that the principle of hierarchical distinctions functioning as marriage rules at the levels of the king and his descendants is attested at least to the third generation. We may assume, therefore, that the same principle also operated in the fourth and fifth generations, the area of marriage between non-kin starting, as we have seen, beyond the fifth generation. The individuals in this last, fifth generation belonged either to Hanan-Cuzco as "great-great-grandsons," or to Hurin-Cuzco as "nephews." Being called "noble commoners" (Betanzos Bk. 1, Ch. 16), they still might claim a royal ancestor. But as they could not trace their descent to an individual mummy, they were in the same position as a commoner in their choice of a spouse. John Earls and Françoise Héritier both have stressed the importance of rules controlling marriage and incest which are superimposed on the more general rule of second-degree cross-cousin marriage. There are some Inca data that corroborate this important observation, but the situation resulting from the application of these other rules is not absolutely clear to me insofar as the Inca marriage system is concerned.[14] I propose, however, to analyze in the third chapter an Inca myth that offers many indications of the distinctions to be made between the fourth and fifth genealogical and hierarchical levels, and of the difference between these levels and those of the *cacacunas,* the affines chosen among the non-kin who constitute a sixth level in addition to the five studied so far.

I have mentioned the existence of still another indigenous version of the model offered by Pérez Bocanegra. Françoise Héritier also makes reference to this version.[15] I will follow her way of genealogical representation, except for small modifications regarding the positions attributed to the king and the queen. The importance of this model derives from the fact that it exemplifies the use of the term "nephew" to designate the "secondary son," a problem that I intend to study here. I want to stress, however, that it is to this model that I will refer later on in more general terms when interpreting the names of the ten districts and their administrators (Fig. 9).[16]

For the study of the Quechua term *concha,* "child of a man's sister" (nephew or niece), it is useful to consider it in the context of the opposition between the term that designates "mother's brother" and the one used for "father's sister." *Caca,* "mother's brother," is also

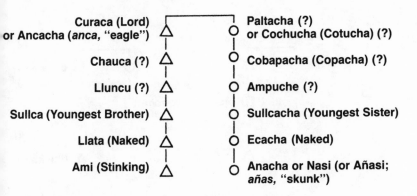

Figure 9. The groups of six "brothers" and six "sisters" (in Huarochiri, according to Francisco de Avila, Ch. 8).

the word used by a man for his male affines; more specifically for the male relatives of a wife who herself was not initially related to her future husband. The postulated equivalence between the wife's brother (or the wife's father) and the mother's brother did not imply cross-cousin marriage. But the term *ipa*, in its social connotation, indicates precisely the opposite. In Aymara (Bertonio), the same word *ipa*, "father's sister," also connotes "the man who in a homosexual relation is in the female position" and is found again in the term *ipapupa*, "drone of the hive." In opposition to the widest possible kinship relation, that between ego and *caca*, we are dealing here with the narrowest possible relation, the one established between ego and *ipa*, a woman belonging to ego's own patriline (Fig. 10).

It is in such a context that the following taxonomic data acquire their full meaning: in Quechua, the father's sister says *mulla* to her brother's child; but this term is also used by the younger brother when addressing his older brother's children. From there, we can also assume that an older brother would call his younger brother's children *concha*, "sister's children." If the king calls the child that he had of a non-Inca woman *huaccha concha*, "poor sister's son," then the position of the said woman becomes that of a sister, and her son finds himself in the position of a younger brother's son. In fact, if we pursue the argument, each younger brother must in turn find himself

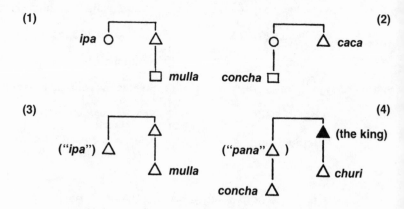

Figure 10. Hypothetical explanation of the term *concha* (man's sister's child), used to designate the secondary son of a man, in order to distinguish him from *churi*, term applied to the older son.

in the position of "sister" of his own older brother. The Quechua word for "man's sister," *pana*, is probably related to the Aymara word *pana*, "second." On the basis of this observation I will later study the word *panaca*, which designates all of the nine noble *ayllus* represented in Figure 6 by cognatic lines, with the exception of the first *ayllu* represented by the central line, the patriline, and which is the Capac Ayllu, the "Royal Ayllu." The possibility offered by the Quechua and Aymara kinship terminology of placing a man in the position of a woman, or vice versa, and the definition of homosexual relationships in Andean societies allow us to clarify the model of the twelve names of brothers and sisters (Fig. 9). I will thus be able to show the importance of this taxonomy for the study of the relations between the noble *ayllus*.[17]

In the model presented in Figure 9, the first brother is called "eagle" or "lord," and the first sister is possibly indicated as "full moon" for "principal lady" or "queen." The names of the fifth-generation brother and sister mean "naked," reminding us of a modern custom, still alive in villages of the southern Andes, where people who have migrated to the cities and return home to visit in their city clothes are referred to as *qala,* "naked" (Mannheim 1986). In addition, there is an important amount of data attesting that the names of so-called "stinking" animals—fox, opossum, skunk, and others—are used to designate non-kin and affinal relatives descending from non-kin. As a preliminary observation, we could say that in comparing this model to Pérez Bocanegra's it is obvious that the fifth and sixth brothers and sisters form a separate group that is recognized as such; and that within the group of the first four, the fourth brother and sister are called *sullca,* "younger or youngest siblings." Unfortunately, we do not know exactly the meaning of the names of the second and third brothers and sisters. But here Pérez Bocanegra comes to our aid. He tells us that the first and second sons are the older brothers who carry on their back the youngest and the smallest (the *sullcas*). Let us consider again the twelve-name system: we will call the first and second generations the generations of the first-born, and the third together with the fourth, that of the younger children. Thus is created among the six generations a tripartite division according to which the *cacacunas,* the affines or relatives through marriage, are incorporated as the sixth generation, but in the quality of "stinkers."[18]

This is where the fact that the older son is a "son" and the younger son a "nephew," together with the concept of ritual homosexuality, helps us to understand another dimension of the distinction between older and younger—a distinction which in turn relates to the opposition between lord and priest, or that between lord and servant in the public services and the temples. Pedro de Cieza de León (1967 Ch. 25; 1945 Ch. 64)—with Betanzos one of the first and most knowledgeable chroniclers on the Incas—says that in the temples lived priests, raised there since childhood, with whom on holidays the lords engaged in homosexual relations. These priests, he adds, dressed like women. Another chronicler (Arriaga 1968 Ch. 3) mentions a temporary priestly function in the context of agricultural rituals, where the man spoke in a female voice. Finally, Rodrigo Hernández Príncipe (pp. 466, 471–474), writing in 1621, gives the details of a case, dating from prehispanic times, where a daughter is sacrificed by her father, lord of several villages, at the occasion of the construction of an irrigation canal. In this narration, the youngest brothers of the sacrificial victim officiated as their sister's priests in time of sowing and harvesting. They exercised these religious functions for their entire lives and transmitted them to their descendants. During the ritual celebrations, these priests spoke in a woman's voice (Zuidema 1977–1978). These three examples concern either a homosexual relation with a priest-servant affiliated to the temple, who was considered as his partner's younger brother and in a female position to him, or the temporary calendrical function of a younger brother who officiated, dressed like a woman, during specific agricultural ceremonies. We will see that in the genealogical and administrative system of Cuzco, it was the younger brothers or cousins, related to the king through their grandfather or great-grandfather—that is to say, men in the position of third and fourth brothers in the twelve-sibling system—who fulfilled the functions of priests during specific agricultural ceremonies. In fact, we have already had the opportunity to observe a similar tripartite division concerning the six genealogical positions given in the origin myth. Manco Capac and his first brother were respectively king and "owner of the land" in Cuzco itself. The two other brothers as priests had remained behind in the region where the Incas contracted exogamous alliances. As for the father and grandfather, they represented the conquered populations.

This rapid comparison with the origin myth of Cuzco underlines the geographical aspect of the model. But we can also stress its purely genealogical side and ask why the relation between the first and second son on the one hand, and the third and fourth on the other has such strong homosexual overtones. Because it is formulated in male terms, this relation acquires a political and hierarchical quality. However, the inequality between the partners gives a female characteristic, related to agriculture, to the one who is in a subservient position. From this we can infer that the king and the high priest, as they are respectively glossed as "son" and "servant" of the Sun (Molina "el Almagrista" pp. 74–76), are themselves in a relation of master to servant. The homosexual relation between rulers and occupants of the land, while implying the notion of alliance, excludes all idea of marriage between them. Furthermore, that practice coexists with the possibility, for the rulers, of contracting symmetrical marriage alliances within a group that excludes priests. It seems to me, nevertheless, that a relation between men symbolized by sexual ties entails a dimension that is more symmetrical and endogamous than any heterosexual relation. What we retain will thus be the primacy given to the symmetrical principle. For, even if we can derive a number of oppositions between, for example, homosexual and heterosexual relations, endogamous and exogamous marriages, or individuals of the same hierarchical level and those of different hierarchical levels, in all these cases it is the principle of symmetry that prevails.

◄ 3 ►

Inca Mythology

I have now reached the point where I can take up the problem of Inca mythology and history. In the second chapter, I established that, from the system of six male names and six female names as found in Huarochiri, it was possible to infer a tripartite division of society: the first and second names corresponded to the group of lords; the third and fourth to the priest-servants; finally, names like "Naked" and "Stinking" applied to the group of fourth-degree relatives and non-kin. This type of division corresponds in Cuzco to that of the names of ancestors identified with past kings, who were also the ancestors in collateral lines of the ten administrators of *chapas*. To this last number can be added the two autochthonous groups who already lived in the valley before the Incas (Zuidema in press b). It would be an error to try to reconstruct an Inca history localized in Cuzco, based on facts that are not in the least "historical" in our sense of the word. Indeed, all these histories of ancestors are derived from mythical models similar to those found in other parts of Peru. The Inca authorities used these tales to account for actual situations, within a contemporary administrative, hierarchical, and geographical context, and not to elucidate historical facts. It is nonetheless obvious that these "histories" can help us to understand how the Incas themselves conceived of their own past.

I propose to consider now two of these myths. In the conclusion, we will be able to look at the problems of historiography faced by the sixteenth-century Spaniards who were trying to decipher this social model in terms of a Western type of royal dynasty. I will also indicate where, in my opinion, the materials can be found for reconstructing Inca ideas about their historical expansion outside the Cuzco Valley. But I will have to leave for later the critique of modern historians who want to see in these Spanish attempts at reconstruction a History conforming to an "objective" chronology and truth. Even if these modern imaginary interpretations do include a few available historical data, they exclude in return a wealth of information that can be derived from a perfectly demonstrable mythical and political structure. Hence we get a narration that claims to be historical and factual, but in fact is merely another myth: a modern one.

Figure ii summarizes the information regarding (1) the names of royal ancestors; (2) the *panacas*—i.e., the noble *ayllus* defined by the *chapa* districts, using the numbering that I have assigned to them previously; and (3) the ten non- or pre-Inca *ayllus* which, in the organization of the *ceque* system, each seem to be associated with a *panaca*.

In my book on Cuzco (1964), as well as in several later articles, I have presented a number of arguments to support the thesis that the names of the ancestors were first and foremost titles that indicated their respective genealogical distance from the reigning king. I concluded that these names could also be used by those of their descendants who occupied the same social rank as their eponymous ancestors. In several cases, the names of the *panaca* and of a non-Inca *ayllu* reflect the personality of the corresponding ancestor. It would seem that the names in Hurin-Cuzco reproduce in a weaker form the name structure found in Hanan-Cuzco. Within terms of the model of Figure ii, the names in the generations of the king and his father would relate to the function of ruler; those in the generations of the grandfather and great-grandfather would refer to religious and agricultural functions; and, finally, the name of the *panaca* Vicaquirao, "Feces (of a Baby) in a Cradle," evokes the great-great-grandfather and would belong to the category of "stinking."

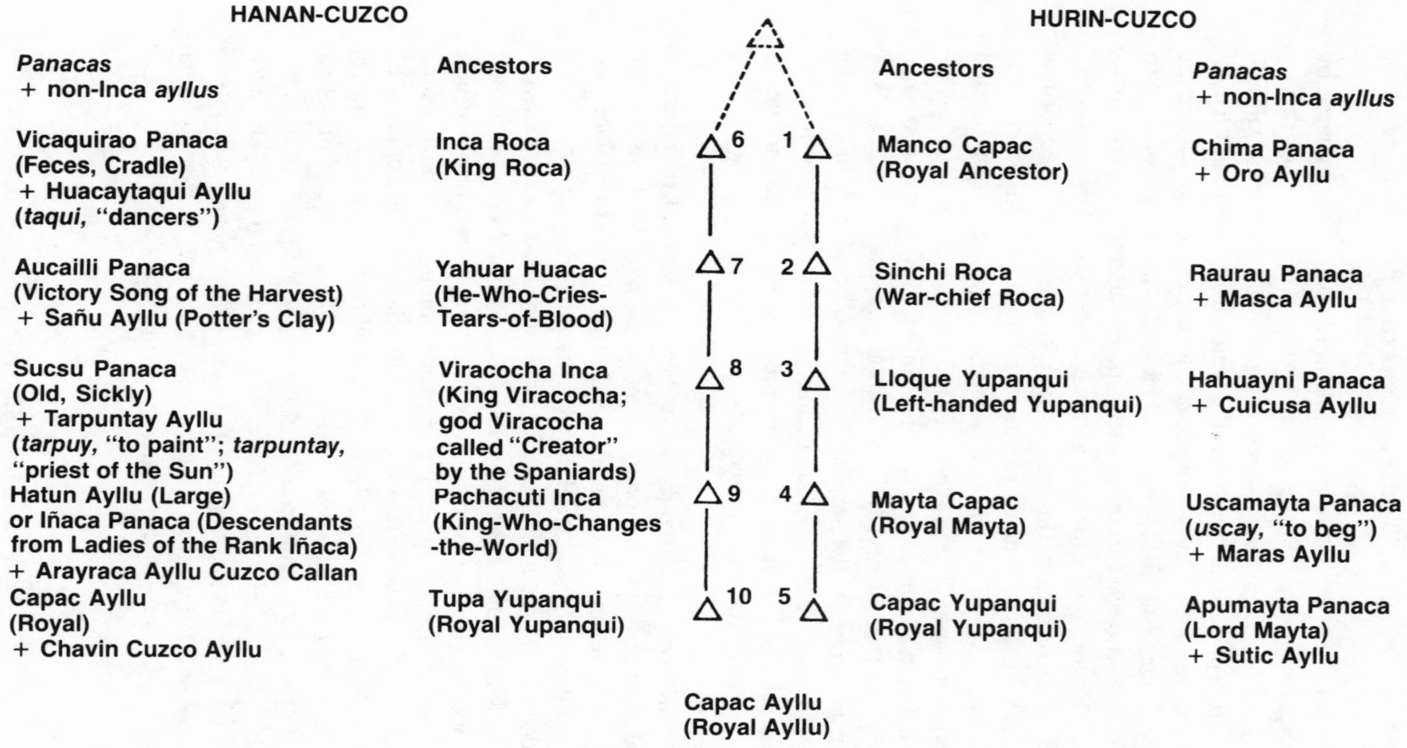

Figure II. The hierarchy of royal ancestors, *panacas* (noble *ayllus*), and *ayllus*.

Tupa Amaru Inca

Coming now to the myths, I will briefly examine the first example: Jeanette E. Sherbondy (1979 59–62; 1982a; 1987 p. 144) and I (1986 [1978]; 1982a) have in several instances already referred to the case. The prince who interests me, Tupa Amaru Inca, "Royal Serpent," was the older son of the organizer-king, Pachacuti Inca, the ninth king of the traditional dynasty. Although Tupa Amaru was supposed to inherit the throne, because of his pacific disposition he was relegated by his father to the role of "second person," or lieutenant, when his younger brother, Tupa Yupanqui, became king. Tupa Amaru, in his role of "second person," replaced the king whenever the latter had to be absent from the capital. When Tupa Yupanqui died, the throne became vacant until Tupa Amaru, who had continued to discharge his duties as "second person," himself died (Molina "el Cuzqueño" 1925 p. 280; Santacruz Pachacuti pp. 247, 254–255). Only then was a new king elected as son of Tupa Yupanqui, thus assuring the succession.

In his role of "second person," Tupa Amaru Inca was in charge of agriculture in Cuzco and thus in direct contact with the lower classes of the population. He was considered—as were the king-priest Viracocha Inca and his namesake the god Viracocha—as the inventor of a very fine type of cloth, decorated with the *tucapu* signs of great heraldic importance (Santacruz Pachacuti p. 242; Sarmiento Ch. 25; Taylor Ch. 1, p. 50). In addition, Tupa Amaru was the organizer of the *huacas,* the sacred sites of the conquered peoples (Murúa Bk. 1, Ch. 20). His connection to agriculture is clearly seen in the following myth: Once there was a dreadful drought that destroyed the whole harvest of the Cuzco Valley. Only Tupa Amaru's lands were spared thanks to the clouds that kept hovering over his fields. Tupa Amaru was then able to store his crop, and to distribute it later to the needy. For this reason, he was worshipped as the inventor of *collcas,* storerooms, and his palace in Cuzco was located in a place known as Collcampata, "Place of the Storehouses; Place Where the Harvest Is Stored" (Santacruz Pachacuti pp. 246–247).

The interest of such mythic narrations resides, first of all, in the fact that they indicate how the administrative rules were put into practice in a given case. In spite of the claim that it was as "second person" of Tupa Yupanqui that Tupa Amaru was put at the head of the Royal Ayllu (Capac Ayllu, no. 10), the other information that we have about him is linked to the *panaca* and the person of his grandfather, the king-priest Viracocha Inca (the ancestor of the eighth *panaca*). The myth of the drought becomes clearer when we analyze it in relation with the March rituals, the time when people await the end of the rainy season and the beginning of the harvest. We are able to locate the lands of Tupa Amaru and the irrigation canal that served them, called the Amaru Canal, "Serpent Canal." They are in Antisuyu (III), near the lands of Sucsu Panaca, associated with Viracocha Inca. When the Spanish conquerors discovered, in an Inca town north of Cuzco, the mummy presumed to have been that of Viracocha Inca, they also found in the same place the stone image, his *huauque,* "brother," called Amaru Inca (Sarmiento Ch. 25; Cobo Bk. 12, Ch. 11). In Inca culture, it was the mummies that established the relations between the living and the *huacas:* stones and sacred places. More specifically, they established the relations between the obligations of the administrative system to replace its civil servants regularly and the system of administrative functions and distribution of land. In this light, the finding of their mummies tells us little about the historical character of the persons identified with them, but much about the social system.

As for the lands known as Amaru's, the colonial documents allow us to reconstruct somewhat the system of Incaic land-rights in this specific instance. For one thing, we know that the lands were worked by people who had been introduced there as *mitimaes* (populations displaced as settlers by the government), and that these *mitimaes* came from the province of the Chancas. (It may in that respect be of interest to note that a myth designates this province as the birthplace of Tupa Amaru [Santacruz Pachacuti p. 242].) The relationship, dating from prehispanic times, between the individual name Tupa Amaru and the lands of Amaru probably came from a territory assigned to an administrative function, and not from inheritance in a given line; this type of right is also attested in other parts of Peru.

Finally, the importance of Tupa Amaru for agriculture and his connection with Viracocha Inca suggest that there existed also a relation between Tupa Amaru and the *ayllu* that joined the *panaca* of Viracocha Inca. It was the *ayllu* called Tarpuntay, "The Planters."

The Myth of Yahuar Huacac

Although the case of Tupa Amaru offers some remarkable possibilities for future research, we had to reconstruct the myth from isolated data, consistent with each other, but emanating from discrete sources. The other example, told in a very detailed way by Sarmiento de Gamboa (Chs. 19–24) in 1572, rather seems to be inspired by a complete myth, analogous in its structure to other Andean myths. If, in its Spanish version, this Inca myth reads like a dynastic story, the others have better preserved their cosmological character. The unity of this group of myths is manifest not only in their structural similarities, but even more in the fact that they fulfill the same calendrical function: they speak of April as the beginning of harvest time, the season when cultivated land is redistributed, when marriage alliances are renewed, and when preoccupations with the future are centered around the agricultural year to come. The myth of Yahuar Huacac (the seventh ancestor, Fig. 11) unfolds at several levels: it informs us about the irrigation system, the political organization around Cuzco, and the relations between the city and the groups of Incas-by-privilege. It is, however, most informative in regard to three types of marriage alliances: that of Inca Roca, the first king of the Hanan dynasty in Cuzco; that of Yahuar Huacac, his son; and finally that of Viracocha Inca, his grandson. It is this aspect of the myth that will now interest us: my aim is to show that, from the point of view of the reigning king, these three types of alliance correspond to the hierarchical levels of great-great-grandfather, great-grandfather, and grandfather, and that together they offer, actualized over three generations, an Inca theory of the political incorporation of the conquered populations into the state as Incas-by-privilege.

The life of Yahuar Huacac, as told in a simplified form in modern works on Inca history, is quite banal. It is used to give a literal explanation of the king's name, "He-Who-Cries-Tears-of-Blood" or "Blood-crying King," referring to his congenital weakness. His father had taken for wife Mama Micay, a native of the villages of Paullu and Pata Huayllacan to the northeast of Cuzco, although she had already been promised to King Tocay Capac of the Ayarmacas (for these place names, see Fig. 1). I have previously mentioned the name of Tocay Capac's capital, Maras, as one of the non- or pre-Inca *ayllus* of Cuzco. In retaliation, Tocay Capac claimed paternity rights over the son that Mama Micay would bear. One day, when the infant Yahuar Huacac was visiting with his maternal relatives, they were forced to surrender the child to Tocay Capac, and this was the reason Yahuar Huacac wept tears of blood. Later, informed by a wife of Tocay Capac, herself from the village of Anta, Inca Roca managed to recover his son Yahuar Huacac. The latter, eventually, once he had become king, formed an alliance with Tocay Capac, taking Tocay Capac's daughter as wife, and giving him his sister in exchange. As for the people of the village of Anta, whence came the woman who had warned Inca Roca, they were declared "relatives-of-the-Incas," and later Viracocha Inca, the son of Yahuar Huacac, married a woman from that group, Mama Runtucaya.

This narrative is given as an aside to various versions of the territorial expansion of the Incas and contains many implausible details from a historical point of view. For example, Sarmiento claims that on several other occasions the people of Pata Huayllacan deceived Inca Roca and Yahuar Huacac: they also betrayed Yahuar Huacac *after* his accession to the throne. If this was true, it seems rather surprising that later, if the chronicles are to be believed, the keeping of the mummy was entrusted precisely to those villages.

But there are also purely mythical elements that are quite as central to our purpose. Thus we read how Mama Micay, coming to Cuzco, discovered that the valley lacked irrigation water. In the myth, she brings water from her own region, for there is near her village of origin a lake, Coricocha, which to this day is thought to supply water to the surrounding villages, although there is no outlet of water to permit this (Sherbondy 1982b). Besides, Cuzco is too far away, and the belief, still alive, of an underground water connection between Lake Coricocha and the Cuzco Valley is, hydrologically speaking, quite impossible. In addition—and this episode is diametrically in opposition to the Mama Micay story—Inca Roca is reputed to have discovered in the valley itself an underground spring, supposedly a resurgence of the river of Cuzco (Zuidema 1986 [1978]). The site of the discovery is well known, and I am rather inclined to interpret the story as the intervention of a mythical giant, of a civilizing hero and representative of the underground world. It is said that formerly the same water would have flowed toward another valley, separated by mountains in the northwest, a valley which at the time reportedly belonged to Tocay Capac's Ayarmacas. Thus the myth offers two conflicting explanations: while in the case of Mama Micay, wife of Inca Roca, we are presented with irrigation water that never could have reached Cuzco, in the case of Inca Roca himself, on the contrary, the water never could have left the valley. Here my reading of the myth is that its purpose is to account for a natural geographical situation, and not to describe conquests. The actions of Inca Roca do not correspond to the functions of a king, but to those of the great-great-grandfather of a king, who, under the circumstances, acts as representative of the social class known as "noble commoners," owners of the water and tillers of irrigated lands. In fact, according to Cobo (Bk. 12, Ch. 9), the regulation of irrigation water in the valley devolved upon the descendants of Inca Roca, and we could conclude that these descendants belonged effectively to the category of classificatory great-great-grandsons of the king, in accordance with Guaman Poma's diagram (Fig. 5).

Moreover, we notice that the myth is interested in toponomy: all the persons mentioned in relation to the villages of Paullu and Pata Huayllacan—namely, Mama Micay; her father, Soma Inca; and even a brother of Inca Roca—were in the sixteenth century well known in the region as so many *huacas* (sacred sites) (Rostworowski 1962).

Considered as a myth of origin, the story of Yahuar Huacac gives a human dimension to a natural geographical situation and invokes the genealogical model to explain this situation as the result of a process leading to the social and ritual integration of the Incas-by-privilege within Inca society. For my part, I will refer to the myth to better understand the operation of the model. The marriage of Yahuar

Huacac occupies an intermediary position between that of his father, Inca Roca, and that of his son, Viracocha Inca, two marriages that are presented as inversions of each other. Yahuar Huacac exchanges his sister for the daughter of Tocay Capac: an exchange operated on an equal footing. As king, Viracocha Inca could demand, as a form of tribute, a wife from a village of Incas-by-privilege, which in this case was identified as one of "relatives-of-the-Incas." But in the case of Inca Roca, the situation is more ambiguous. Although it is tempting to interpret his case from the perspective of the apparent superiority of the Incas, certain aspects reveal his true position—one of inferiority—which is also the position of Cuzco vis-à-vis the region of Paullu and Pata Huayllacan, and not the other way round. We note, for instance, that Inca Roca had to leave his son as hostage in that region, and that Cuzco was dependent on the same region for its water supply. And this state of subordination can even be seen in the name of the *panaca* associated with Inca Roca: Soma Panaca, a name that Gutiérrez de Santa Clara, in his account of the administrative system (Vol. 3, Ch. 50, p. 211) attributes to this noble *ayllu,* which would thus be named for Inca Roca's father-in-law, the father of Mama Micay.

In conclusion, the story of the three generations can be interpreted in terms of a political evolution: from an initial position of inferiority, Cuzco would have reached a situation of superiority, through an intermediary stage of equality. The three regions under consideration (Paullu–Pata Huayllacan, Maras, and Anta) are of comparable importance, and their distance to Cuzco more or less equal. This is therefore not a case of strategic expansion, of conquests, but rather a process of political integration. Seen from this angle, the first marriage presents the most exogamous character, the third is the most endogamous, while the second appears as an example of balanced, symmetrical exchange. If the myth presents these marriages as so many royal marriages, it is because it takes the perspective of the cognatic descendants for whom those kings figure as their eponymous ancestors.

In addition, the myth needs to be understood in terms of the relations of the king to his subjects, and of the subjects among themselves, at the time of the year when the harvest from the surrounding villages is brought into town, and when the redistribution of land takes place.[19] This is what is expressed in the calendrical position occupied by Yahuar Huacac's *panaca* (see Chapter 5), and even in the name itself: Aucailli Panaca; *aucailli* meaning "victory song of the harvest."

My purpose here has been to demonstrate that we are really dealing with a myth, and not a narration with a claim to historicity. I relied on the myth to explain the regional political situation of Cuzco. I still need to analyze the structure of the central theme, in order to clarify the position it occupies in the context of similar myths in Peru and elsewhere. I will conclude my analysis with a rapid comparison of the Yahuar Huacac myth with a myth from Central Peru, published and studied by Pierre Duviols (1974–1976 pp. 275–278, 288–290).

In my opinion, the myth of Yahuar Huacac essentially deals with the following themes: two men fight over the hero's paternity, one because the child's mother had been promised to him in marriage, and the other because he is indeed the child's actual begetter; Yahuar Huacac, the hero, lives successively in four distinct places; as a child, he is the victim of an abduction and cries tears of blood; and finally, for his family, these four changes of residence are so many occasions to contract marriage alliances.

In the other myth, the one presented by Duviols, two men, Tumayricapa and his brother—they are probably twins—come down from heaven as the sons of the Thunder God. This event takes place near Lake Chinchaycocha (today Lake Junin), in a place called Mamallqui Jirca, which means, according to the myth itself, "plant or principle or origin of the mountains." Tumayricapa gathers all the *huacas*, the sacred places or mountains, and then goes on to a plain where he changes into an infant. A woman hears him cry at dawn, takes him home, and breastfeeds him. Five days later, he has regained adult size. Once more, he summons the mountains, challenges them to a great battle, and defeats them. Then he goes down to two places where people live. He welcomes those of the valley of Huánuco, and seals his acceptance of them as "nephews" by cutting the hair of their children born during the previous year; in other terms, he behaves toward them as a "maternal uncle," to whom befalls this first cutting, followed by further cuttings performed by the relatives of the father. This done, Tumayricapa visits the people of another locality, Yanamata, where he is recognized as "father."

The custom of cutting the hair of children born the previous year, linked to the gesture of putting the child down on the ground for the first time, was also known in other parts of Peru. Bertonio mentions it, for instance, for the Titicaca region.[20] It was a rite performed at the end of the harvest, and as part of it. In addition, it looks as if the myth mentions this ritual in order to explain why some people are known as "sons" and others as "nephews." We find that a social division, recognized in Cuzco at the level of great-great-grandsons of the king, that is to say at the hierarchical level of those who worship Inca Roca as their great-great-grandfather, is expressed in Chinchaycocha as a social division decreed by a god: the Thunder God. This god was the object of a particular cult on the part of twins, and it is in relation to him that twice in the myth the theme occurs of the duality or redoubling of the hero. Tumayricapa comes to earth together with his brother; he also has two mothers: the first one—the mountain called "plant or principle or origin of the mountains"—is his natural mother; the second—the woman who, at dawn, breastfeeds him when he cries—is the mother who restores him to his adult size.[21] The myth brings together the three themes that we recognized in the Yahuar Huacac myth: the redoubling of the father, the crying child, and the reorganization of space. A comparison between the two myths might lead us to assimilate Tumayricapa, the child who cries and is destined to be reborn, to Yahuar Huacac, "He-Who-Cries-Tears-of-Blood," abducted as a child and later returned to Cuzco, where he too is "reborn." But this comparison can also suggest that Cuzco is opposed to the surrounding villages, just as, in Chinchaycocha, "sons" are opposed to "nephews." It is in that perspective that the myth of Yahuar Huacac, beginning with the generation of Inca Roca and ending with that of Viracocha Inca, seems to lay the principle, or indicate the origin, of the division in Cuzco between the "great-great-grandsons" and the *huaccha concha,* the "nephews," within the social class known as "noble commoners."

The Incas and History

I believe that the analysis of material such as the myths of Tupa Amaru Inca and Yahuar Huacac can lead to an understanding of how the Incas themselves perceived the functioning of the social, hierarchical, and genealogical model which Las Casas, Gutiérrez, and Guaman Poma described. The last myth helped us to understand the place of the first three generations in this model and the first that of the next two. In addition, these myths make it possible to interpret more accurately the documents relating to the toponyms they mention. I still need to indicate briefly how in my opinion colonial historiography was able to incorporate this kind of information in its reconstruction of a dynastic history—a reconstruction that clearly was and remains totally hypothetical.

We began the tentative reconstruction of the myths keeping in mind the model given in Figures 6 and 11. We now realize that the two brother-ancestors, as they were situated at each genealogical level, do not, in fact, designate true brothers, but rather cousins, and that their genealogical distance to each other is equal to their respective distance from the reigning king.

In a first stage, Spanish chroniclers perceived the ancestors of the various cognatic lines as kings belonging to two parallel dynasties: one reigning over Hanan-Cuzco and the other over Hurin-Cuzco (Zuidema 1964; Duviols 1979). From the genealogical model established above, we notice that the ancestors in Hurin-Cuzco did not follow each other in a "straight" patrilineal line, but that the succession went from one *huaccha concha*—a king's "poor nephew"—to another. But the concept of two parallel dynasties precludes such a characteristic and attributes to Hurin-Cuzco a mode of dynastic succession similar to that of Hanan-Cuzco. In a second stage, the whole Hurin dynasty was seen as predating the Hanan dynasty, on the basis of hierarchical differences expressed in kinship terms. This new view did not necessarily oblige the Spaniards to consider the dynastic model of Inca society as less hierarchical, because, in fact, the hierarchical relations between the moieties and between the ancestral kings themselves remained the same.

This two-stage process was only a first aspect of the evolution that would lead the Spaniards to accept the existence of what was apparently a historical dynasty. The memory of the Inca informants, who after the Conquest referred to the kings they personally had known, further contributed to the evolution of the Spaniards' perception of the model. The kings who were mentioned to the Spaniards from personal memories were Huascar and Atahuallpa, fighting their fratricidal war at the time of the Conquest, and their father, Huayna Capac. With their grandfather, Tupa Yupanqui, the tenth king in our genealogical model, we already lose such immediate control over our data.

Having arrived at this point of the argument, it is important to be aware of the fact that the whole royal function was limited to Capac Ayllu, the Royal Ayllu (no. 10). All the kings who truly had ruled, as well as all the high nobility, belonged to this *ayllu*. Although the later reconstruction of the dynastic model, made by the Spaniards, mentions Pachacuti Inca (no. 9) as father of Tupa Yupanqui (no. 10) and as grandfather of Huayna Capac, there are various reasons to doubt that he was only two generations removed from the latter. For two of these reasons the name and role of the person called Capac Yupanqui are especially illustrative.

First, Capac Yupanqui is mentioned as a secondary son of Pachacuti Inca by a secondary wife (Betanzos Bk. 1, Ch. 20) and as the last king (no. 5) in Hurin-Cuzco. As his name itself is a synonym of Tupa Yupanqui (no. 10), "Royal Yupanqui," we may wonder if the two different persons called Capac Yupanqui did not fulfill similar or identical roles in the hierarchical order of Inca administration. In the model of the two contemporaneous dynasties of Hanan and Hurin, Capac Yupanqui would have been the Hurin king, next to Tupa Yupanqui as the Hanan king, while in the single dynastic sequence he had the role of commander of the Inca army next to Tupa Yupanqui (Zuidema 1964 pp. 129–133). It is thus quite possible that events that had happened to Capac Yupanqui, the son of Pachacuti Inca, were transferred to the king Capac Yupanqui, four generations earlier. One early chronicle (Castro and Ortega y Morejón p. 237), reporting on the coastal valley of Chincha, even mentions that, according to the view of its inhabitants, Capac Yupanqui, in fact, was the father of Tupa Yupanqui!

The second reason for doubt is that in different examples of rulers or generals after Pachacuti Inca the same name is given to two persons, one succeeding the other. Thus, it was said that a particular incident had not happened to a first person with the name of Capac Yupanqui in the time of Pachacuti Inca but to a second (Zuidema 1964 p. 131, n. 44). Similarly, José de Acosta (Bk. 6, Ch. 21) mentions of another incident how it had involved Tupa Yupanqui, not the first person of that name, but the second. Apparently, there were two kings of that name, one succeeding the other!

The recently edited complete version of the chronicle of Betanzos (1987) allows us now to account for this kind of dispersed data in a more tightly argued way. Given the early time that he wrote (1551) and the introduction he had to Inca society through his marriage to an Inca princess who was the former promised wife of Atahuallpa, Betanzos perhaps had a better and more realistic understanding of Inca dynastic problems than anybody after him. Two new issues are of importance to us. First he says (Bk. 1, Ch. 20, pp. 100–101) that Pachacuti Ynga Yupangue, as crowned king, had two sons, Yamque Yupangue and Topa Ynga Yupangue, by his principal wife, the queen, and a third son, Capac Yupangue, by another wife. He celebrated the births of all three princes with large feasts. Then he took as wives twenty other noble women who belonged to Hanan- and to Hurin-Cuzco. From the way in which Betanzos (Bk. 1, Ch. 8, p. 32; Ch. 16, p. 75) uses the number 20, we may conclude that ten of these wives belonged to Hanan and ten to Hurin.

Betanzos returns to what apparently is the same issue at the occasion of the death of Pachacuti Inca (Bk. 1, Ch. 32, p. 150). Yamque Yupanqui, who was much older than his brother Tupa Yupanqui, succeeded his father when the latter abdicated and then ruled independently as crowned king. But Pachacuti Inca lived on—although he became senile—till he was 120 years old, and Tupa Yupanqui did not fully succeed his brother until the latter died shortly after the death of Pachacuti Inca at a more normal age of 85 years (Betanzos Bk. 1, Ch. 36). All the descendants of Pachacuti Inca were called "*Ca*-

pac aillo Ynga Yupangue haguaymin, which means of the lineage of kings' descendants and grandchildren of *Ynga Yupangue*" (Betanzos Bk. 1, Ch. 32). But many of these descendants married women who were not "of the same lineage," and thus they were forced to adopt other surnames. We can conclude that both Yamque Yupanqui and Tupa Yupanqui belonged to Capac Ayllu and that the other nine *panacas* represented the other members of Inca nobility who had adopted other surnames, in Hanan- as well as in Hurin-Cuzco. According to this version of Betanzos, then, all the *panacas* were descendants of Pachacuti Inca!

Betanzos interprets the succession of Pachacuti Inca as if Yamqui Yupanqui and Tupa Yupanqui were brothers. He applies an Inca rule of succession in Cuzco that was known also for the succession of *curacas* elsewhere: an eldest brother was succeeded first by his younger brother(s) and only then by his son.[22] But the fact that Pachacuti Inca's lifespan really was that of two men and not of one might also be interpreted in another way. We are dealing with three generations, but as Yamque Yupanqui and Tupa Yupanqui both belonged to Capac Ayllu, they were in that sense considered as "*ayllu*-brothers" and Pachacuti Inca had to be assigned an improbably old age.[23]

Yamque Yupanqui had a son of the same name, who was also the ancestor of Atahuallpa's promised wife, the woman who later became Betanzos' wife. Betanzos had a clear purpose in mind in elaborating upon the political interests of his wife's family. But the way he discusses that genealogical problem also reminds us very much of that of Tupa Amaru according to other chroniclers. All these data on Capac Yupanqui, Tupa Yupanqui, Yamque Yupanqui, and Tupa Amaru lead us to conclude that more than one generation was involved in between Pachacuti Inca and Huayna Capac. In the context of the ancestral dynasty, Pachacuti Inca and Tupa Yupanqui were still represented by a *panaca* and a *chapa* in the Cuzco Valley, but Huayna Capac no longer was. The first two of these kings and their *panacas* not only represented the end of the territorial and mythical interests in the valley, but also initiated an interest in the mythical origins of the real Inca dynasty. Betanzos reports meticulously the periods of months and years in between many actions of Pachacuti Inca and those of his descendants. With these data at hand it might be possible to reconstruct how he understood his informants on Inca history from Pachacuti Inca on. Thus we might reconstruct an imperial history of Inca expansion (Zuidema 1973a), as separate from the mythical past in the Cuzco Valley which was of more interest for an understanding of Cuzco's calendrical rituals.

In retrospect we become aware that the ahistorical character of the information on the royal ancestors, at least those before Tupa Yupanqui, was not completely lost to some of the later chroniclers. Garcilaso de la Vega, publishing his *Comentarios reales* in 1609, is a good example. First we should be aware that when he includes an extra king, Inca Yupanqui, in his dynasty, in between Pachacuti Inca and Tupa Yupanqui, while maintaining one *panaca* for the first and the second of these kings, he is closer to the truth than originally was assumed. But even though he sketches a utopian picture of Inca expansion beginning long before Pachacuti Inca, he himself (Bk. 7, Ch. 9)[24] expresses clearly his doubt about the historicity of all these former kings in the following words:

> . . . it was in this broad space (of the city) that the Incas of the royal
> blood lived, divided into their *aillus* or clans, though all of them
> were of the same blood and stock. Although they all descended from
> King Manco Cápac, yet each claimed descent from the one or other
> of the kings, saying these descend from this Inca, those from that
> Inca, and so on for all the rest. This is what the Spanish historians
> refer to when they say confusedly that such and such an Inca founded
> one line, and another a different one, suggesting that these were different
> stocks. But the lineages were in fact all the same, as the Indians
> show when they apply the common name *Cápac Aillu*, "august
> lineage of the royal blood," to them all.

Even a writer like Cobo, who did his research in the early seventeenth century but did not finish writing his chronicle until 1653, seems to have had his doubts when he wondered why the earlier kings belonged to Hurin and the later ones to Hanan. He said (Bk. 12, Ch. 8):

... although the Incas who now live in Cuzco have much to say about the kings that belonged to each "*parcialidad*" (= moiety), nevertheless they cannot explain the reason for this distinction; nor could Don Alonso, grandson of Guayna Capac and son of Paullu Inca, satisfy my doubt, with whom I dealt much about Inca matters and other antiquities.

It seems that only when the organization of the *panacas* and the *chapas* lost its importance for discussions about the Inca dynasty did the latter obtain its fully historical perspective in European writings.[25]

4

Female Organization and the Age-Classes

Even though, in my discussion of Inca mythology, I paid little attention to the problems of historical reconstruction, I do remain convinced of the necessity for a historical study, but following radically different methods. I mentioned the villages of Paullu and Pata Huayllacan, and it might be of interest to know that in that region we find an abundance of pre-Incaic archaeological remains, but little evidence of the Incas, who instead settled just across the river, in Pisac. The myth, however, clearly establishes a relation, both political and ritual, between Cuzco and Paullu and Pata Huayllacan. Apparently, representatives of these villages played a particular role in Cuzco during the harvest ritual and were related to lands in the *panaca* known as Aucailli, the *panaca* of Yahuar Huacac. They identified themselves with the lands of that *panaca* when they appeared at the court of the king.

The organization of the ten ancestors was closely related to the organization of space in the Cuzco Valley and was also grounded in a hierarchical model, explicitly formulated in genealogical terms. Now that we have built a more solid base for this kind of discussion, we can consider other renderings of this hierarchical model. Although the social distance between an individual and the king was usually marked in reference to a common ancestor, this does not necessarily indicate a true genealogical distance between the king and the said individual. The latter could very well have achieved his social position through other, more personal means: athletic achievements during initiation rituals; acts of courage during war; administrative competence; the fact that he himself or his mother had been struck by lightning; or even some physical disability.

This is the type of problem that I intend to give priority to as I orient the discussion toward the analysis of age-classes in Inca society, a form of organization which, in spite of its manifest importance, has never received the attention it deserves, with the exception of one study by J. H. Rowe (1958).

One can contrast, in the structuring of an individual's lifetime, two types of organization. Rowe studied the organization of the classes that mark the physical development of the individual, from birth to death. My purpose is different. I am interested here in the internal organization of the class of married adults, from the birth of their first child to the birth of their first grandchild, that is to say the internal organization of one generational span; a type of organization that had among the Incas its own independent structure.[26]

In view of the argument that I intend to develop here, and for a number of other considerations, the information given by Guaman Poma (pp. 298–300 [300–302]) on the age-class system of the "Virgins of the Sun" is of crucial importance. The first reason for considering his data relates to the "horizontal" aspect of the genealogical model that I was able to reconstruct with the help of the origin myth of Manco Capac and his brothers and sisters, and of the information given by Las Casas, Guitérrez, and Guaman Poma on the administration of the *chapas*. This "horizontal" aspect of the model leads us to a problem of kinship that can be formulated in the following terms: how is the four-generation group comparable to the group of four brothers and four sisters?

My hypothesis is this: the four sons or daughters born of a marriage—the last of the four being *sullca*, "youngest"—occupied, in the order of their births, from first to fourth, the period of one twenty-year generation, so that each child represented a five-year age-class. Thus the fifth and sixth children were born at a time when their parents were at an age when they could have, or effectively did have, grandchildren. Nowadays, such children are sometimes called "those who have fallen off the bed," that is "those born after the time when the parents should normally have stopped having children."[27] The age-classes appear, therefore, as so many subdivisions within the generations, and can be treated as such. I have previously evoked the names of six brothers and six sisters mentioned by the chronicler Avila (see Fig. 9). Today the idea is still quite popular in Andean culture that a couple should have twelve children. As a commentary, I would like to mention how Billie Jean Isbell, in a recent manuscript called "The Ethnographic Context for Acquiring and Transforming Andean Culture" (1983), treats the theme of the twelve children. Her study clearly illustrates the ethnographic background of my hypothesis. According to the author, "It is worth pointing out that Andean women expect to have as many as twelve pregnancies, many of which terminate in miscarriages or abortions." "The number of pregnancies numbered six to twelve." " . . . the average number of children who had survived past the age of five, numbered three to five." "Women nurse for about two years, and since they usually spend the intervening time pregnant, many women reach menopause having experienced very few menstrual cycles." An ancient ritual, known as *allusca*, marked the end of the breastfeeding period, which could last two or three years (Sarmiento Ch. 13; Garcilaso Bk. 4, Chs. 11, 12). If conditions comparable to those described by Isbell prevailed in Inca times, a distribution of four children in twenty years would have corresponded to an age-class system of five years each.

The second reason that induces us to study the age-classes as they are described by Guaman Poma concerns the problem of individual status within the social group. We will use the general comparison, the merit of which we have recognized above, between the six age-classes and the six hierarchically ranked social classes. The data provided by modern ethnological studies of the *cargo* system, the hierarchical system of functions through which any married individual must pass, still clearly support the general rule according to which members of the upper social strata are more likely to accede to the highest *cargo* than are those of the lower ones (e.g., B. J. Isbell 1978, Ch. 4). We only have one piece of information from an ancient little chronicle about the way in which prehispanic Andean society established a formal connection between the hierarchical organization and age-classes. Damián de la Bandera (1965) relates the following fact:

during the ceremonies of collective weddings in any given political unit, performed in the presence of a representative of the king, all the individuals to be married were divided into five age-classes of five years each. In terms of this system, the *curaca*, the local chief, who apparently was also involved, was assigned to the last age-class, the oldest one.

The study of the age-classes of the "Virgins of the Sun"—and this is the third reason that incites us to examine their case—leads us to consider the various classificatory models assigned to women, and the various uses they were put to in the Andean sociopolitical system; for instance, in spatial and political divisions, marriage alliances, the calendar, and many other contexts. Against this background, the word *panaca* (derived from *pana*, "sister of a man") which designates nine of the noble *ayllus*, with the one exception of Capac Ayllu, the Royal Ayllu proper, will take on a richer meaning.

Finally, the information given by Guaman Poma allows for a more precise formulation of a problem that I consider fundamental: that of the modalities of applying a cognatic kinship system, such as the one of the Incas, to a given society. Inca society, as it can be observed in Cuzco, included various forms of hierarchical organization that were, in part or in their totality, parallel to one another. Two individuals could occupy the same social position for different reasons and by means of different hierarchical arrangements: in consideration of the position and ranking of a non-Inca mother, or of an Inca one, or else because of the birth-ranking of the individual within the group. These three coexisting, parallel modes of organization were in addition ranked according to a value order: the inside was considered superior and the outside inferior.

I will start my discussion of the age-classes with a reference to more general notions concerning female classifications.[28] In his Aymara dictionary, Bertonio offers some fascinating information concerning the circumstances marking the birth of a girl: whether she was born in times of weddings or when a house was built (under *huampaña*, *pircajaña*), in the fields or on the road (under *pacoma*, *thaquijaña*), etc.; all these circumstances of time and space could be incorporated in the name given to the child. This is also why Inca society attached much importance to female names. All the girls belonging to one age group were selected and divided into classes according to criteria of beauty and physical perfection. The first selection was made among young girls under nine (Cobo Bk. 12, Ch. 34). For five years, they were taught the art of weaving, that of brewing beer, and other skills. After this period of five years, the best among them were sent to a provincial capital. It is from among these "chosen girls," or *acllas,* that were selected the "*acllas* of the Sun"—"of the idols," says Guaman Poma—who for the duration of their lives would remain virgins and undertake the service of the temples. The other girls assumed the title of "*acllas* of the Inca," that is of the king. The most beautiful among these could be distributed as primary or secondary wives to relatives of the Inca or other favored individuals. The administrators in charge of the selection were called Apu Panaca, "Lord Panaca," a title in which we recognize the word *panaca* that in Cuzco designates noble *ayllus.*

The reason for the dual connotation of the word *panaca* can probably be found in relation to this system of repartition of women. The men who were being honored through this distribution were ranked either according to their own genealogical order within the hierarchy, or according to their rank as heads of groups numbering 10, 50, 100, 500, 1,000, 5,000, 10,000, 20,000 and finally 40,000 families. The most highly valued women were attributed to the chiefs, or *curacas,* of 1,000 families and up.

Although only Pedro Pizarro (pp. xlvii, 47, 65–66, 93–95)—one of the first conquerors, and perhaps the best-informed chronicler on female organization—says so explicitly,[29] it seems that there was a narrow relation between the organization of the houses of *acllas,* selected for their beauty, and that of the houses where the primary wives of the king or of a high-ranking *curaca* controlled the execution of the female tasks performed by the women who were considered as secondary wives of the king or *curaca.* Thus there were *acllahuasis,* "houses of the *acllas,*" intended for "*acllas* of the Sun," and others reserved to the "*acllas* of the Inca." Given such information, it is possible to suggest the hypothesis that the houses of the "*acllas* of the Inca" of different ranks were related to the origin of the *panacas* of different ranks within Cuzco itself. These *panacas* are represented as so many cognatic lines. At the center of the whole system lies Capac Ayllu, the only noble *ayllu* never to be called *panaca,* and the following *ayllu* is the only one that bears two distinct names: Hatun Ayllu and Iñaca Panaca (Fig. 11). *Iñaca* is the keyword of the *panaca* system, and I will end my discussion of the social organization with an initial analysis of this word. For the time being, it is important to note that just as the word *concha,* "child of a man's sister," in general designates the sons of kings establishing the various cognatic lines, in the same way the word *panaca,* "group descending from a man's sisters," designates the king's secondary children. The terms *concha* and *panaca* refer to the same groups of people, although *concha* was never used with a qualifier like those used to distinguish the *panacas* from one another.

The selection process of the *acllas* underlines two elements: the girls were classified and grouped according to their beauty, and the Apu Panaca came back every five years to direct the selection. These two elements—the criterion invoked and the periodicity of the act— are narrowly related. Before going into the study of the female age-classes described by Guaman Poma, I would like to point out the information on feminine beauty given by Bertonio in his Aymara dictionary. He mentions under *paco hakhlla* the four following adjectives:

paco hakhlla ("reddish-brown *aclla*"), "a beautiful girl";

hanko hakhlla ("white *aclla*"), "even more beautiful";

huayrur, "the most beautiful girl" (from *huayruru,* a red and black fruit shaped like a bean); [30]

and finally:

haua tahuaco, "the other girls, not beautiful, who had some imperfection that blemished them." They were the excluded ones, for *tauaco* means "girls of over eighteen" and *haua,* "badly made."

The semantic field, in Aymara, of the words *paco* and *hanco* provides some valuable information concerning the underlying social context that determines the names of the *acllas. Paco,* for a boy, and *pacoma,* for a girl, were the names given to children born "when the father or the mother were occupied with a specific task." *Pacoma* or *sullcoma* also meant "prisoner of war or slave" and "any person who has no freedom of movement, to go when and where he wants." Prisoners were assimilated to girls, *pacomas,* and by a similar process of identification, during the army's triumphal entrance into Cuzco, war prisoners had to wear long dresses, like women (Sarmiento Chs. 33, 37; Murúa Bk. 1, Chs. 41, 42; Collapiña p. 48). In addition, in the compound term *hankoyapu*, *hanko*, "white," takes the meaning of "fertile land," and we can conclude that *hanko* itself contained a notion of fertility. *Huayruru* is still frequently used today to designate the highest category in any female classification, for instance in the case of corn or potato seeds.

Moving now to the question of the age-classes, the term *huayrur*

The classes of *acllas* ("the chosen ones") who do not speak with men

1. **Twenty years old and above: the first (class)** *guayrur [huayrur] aclla*, **"the most chosen** *acllas*,**" who enter at twenty and serve the Sun, the Moon, and the Stars, Chasca Coyllur, "Venus of the Morning," and Chuqui Ylla, "Thunder." "Never throughout their lives did they speak to men."**

2. **Thirty and above:** *sumac aclla*, **"the beautiful** *acllas*.**" "They entered at thirty and stayed in that class (of** *acllas*) **until their death." Virgins of the** *huaca* **of Uanacauri, idol of the Incas. "They did not sin, and had no commerce with men."**

3. **Twenty-five and above:** *guayrur aclla sumac*, **"the acllas (between)** *guayrur acllas* **and** *sumac acllas*.**" Virgins of the** *huacas*, **the principal idols. "They are perpetual virgins until death."**

The classes of *acllas* who spin and weave clothes

4. **Thirty-five and above:** *sumac aclla catiquin*, **"who follow the** *sumac acllas*.**" They serve the secondary** *huacas*. **"They spun and wove the clothes of the** *huacas*, **the idols of this kingdom, clothes that were as fine as silk."**

5. **Forty and above:** *aclla chaupi catiquin sumac aclla*, **"the beautiful** *acllas* **who follow the central** *acllas*.**" Virgins of the** *huacas*, **the minor idols. "They participated in the planting and (wove) clothes."**

6. **Fifty and above:** *pampa acllaconas*, **"all the other** *acllas* **of the common people" (***pampa*, **"plain"). They serve the Moon, the Stars, and the other** *huaca*-idols, **the common gods. "They wove the** *chunbes*, **'belts,'** *huinchas*, **'bands,'** *chuspa uatus*, **'strings of the coca pouch,' and** *chuspa ystalla*, **'women's purses.'"**

Figure 12. The age-classes of the *acllas* of the "idols" (or of the Sun), according to Guaman Poma.

is also applied by Guaman Poma to the *acllas* of the highest category, and he uses the word *sumac,* "beautiful," to characterize all the others. For the rest, however, his system is quite different from that of Bertonio. Obviously, both authors use beauty as a criterion, but Guaman Poma expresses these distinctions in relation to age-classes beyond the age of eighteen, i.e., twenty and above. The classes are listed in Figure 12.

"The *acllas* of these six classes," says Guaman Poma, "were all daughters of noble Incas *Auquicunas,*" which is to say daughters of royal blood, down to the king's great-great-granddaughters, and to the *conchas,* his nieces.

Reading this description of age-classes, one gets the rather curious feeling that, from the top to bottom, a noble *aclla* tumbles down all the rungs of the social ladder. But obviously what Guaman Poma intends to say is something quite different. He suggests a correspondence between the six female age-classes and the six male genealogical ranks. Furthermore, he stipulates that the *acllas* of a certain rank "enter" the system at a specific age, but does not indicate whether after five years they move on to the next class. It is possible to think that the first age-class, that of the *acllas* of the Temple of the Sun, belonged to the same genealogical rank as did the king and the queen; a fact that is confirmed by another chronicler, Cristóbal de Molina.[31] Those *acllas* then had to enter the service of the temple at twenty. The women belonging to the genealogical level, or to the cognatic line, of the king's father, entered the service of the *huacas* at twenty-five. The system of succession of age-classes functioned according to the same diagram for the daughters of the other cognatic lines. From this information, we can understand why, for instance, the women who were at the bottom of the hierarchy, in the very last class—that of the pre- or non-Inca *ayllus* of the valley—were only admitted as *acllas* after they had had children and when, being widowed, they were not able to remarry. After the age of fifty, they were only allowed to weave belts and strings.

Another piece of information given by Guaman Poma deserves our attention: it is only the women of the first three classes that he claims were not allowed to talk to men; on the other hand, he describes the other three classes in relation to a very interesting hierarchization applied to textiles. The finest textiles are reserved to the fourth age-class, the coarser ones to the fifth, and to the sixth age-class were entrusted belts and strings and other such items.

We now need to consider in more detail the names of the six classes of *acllas* and the functions fulfilled by each of them, as it is from this angle that we shall be able to elucidate the whole hierarchical system of spatial, political, and religious classifications. Indeed, it all works as if the system used the women, the *acllas*, to indicate, or perhaps to underline, the different steps of these various ranking structures. This observation, by the way, also applies to the Ge Indians, for instance the Eastern Timbira or Canellas, in regard to their moiety divisions, localized plaza groups and societies, and age-classes (Nimuendajú 1946).

After the first class, the one called *huayrur,* come four classes with the word *sumac,* "beautiful," in their names, three of these being five-year classes and one, the fifth class, covering ten years. Finally the sixth and last class, followed by no other until death, shows by its name, *pampa,* "plain, empty space" its opposition to all the other classes; these latter are all connected with inhabited places. The third class (25–30 years), which, because of its age, mediates between the first and the second class, bears a name that combines *huayrur* and *sumac.* The class sequence is animated by a double forward motion followed by a single backward one. Finally, there are two classes that "follow," and that are, in one way or another, classes of "servants": the fourth class (35–40) follows the second (30–35), and the fifth class (40–50) follows the third (25–30). But this last class, because of its dual name—*huayrur* **and** *sumac*—was also likely to have been a class of "followers" of the first class. From these observations, we can diagram the hierarchical order as shown in Figure 13.

There are three hierarchical levels and two columns. At the tops of the columns are respectively the *huayrur acllas* and the *sumac acllas.* The columns themselves are also hierarchically ranked. There are four age-classes of five years each and the other two are of ten years or more. But if we take together, as consecutive classes in each column, the first with the third and the second with the fourth age-classes, then we arrive at yet another structure, this one of four ten-year classes.

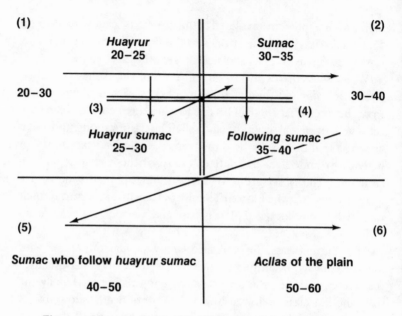

Figure 13. The age-class model of the *acllas* of the Sun. (The short arrows indicate the sequence of the five-year age-classes; the long arrows indicate the sequence of the ten-year age-classes.)

The temporal organization is thus presented to us as a series of blocks embedded in one another. The process of subdivision starts with a series of two consecutive generations that are divided into four ten-year age-classes. The two upper ten-year classes reproduce, in their internal organization, another subdivision into four classes of five years each. To these four are added, however, the two lower ten-year classes as the fifth and sixth. The same process of embedding can be observed in the spatial organization, leading to an effect that in my book on Cuzco (1964) I had called the three "representations" of the city.

This information, drawn from Guaman Poma, gives us not only the best abstract model to understand the spatio-temporal process, but also the best explanatory diagram for the general organization of the system. Applying the model to the spatial organization of the city, with its four *suyus* and its ten noble *ayllus,* I intend to show that here again we are dealing with the same process.

The Spatio-temporal Organization of Cuzco

Let us start with the analysis of this embedding process. We will recognize the process in action—this will be the first phase—in the relation that is established between the age-classes and the spatial organization of the four *suyus* in Cuzco. We recall the distinction between the *huayrur acllas,* who are the *acllas* of the Sun, and the *sumac acllas,* who are the *acllas* of Mount Huanacauri. The spatial relation between the Sun and Huanacauri suggests two types of organization: one concentric and the other diametrical. In regard to the first type, we must point out that the *acllas* of the Sun are identified with the Temple of the Sun, in the center of Cuzco, whereas one of the qualities attributed to Huanacauri in the origin myth was its liminal position at the horizon of the valley. If we admit that this concentric relation between the temple and the mountain is represented by the relation between the *acllas* of 20 to 30 years and those of 30 to 40, we can conclude that the two remaining age-classes—the ones of 40 to 50 and 50 to 60 and above—represent the space beyond the limits of the valley.

In addition, the Temple of the Sun, although it was built at the center of Cuzco, was perceived as belonging to Chinchaysuyu (I), whereas Mount Huanacauri, the foremost *huaca* in the whole valley, belonged to Collasuyu (II). In this perspective, which is diametrical but still open to the outside, we can consider that:

the *acllas* of age 20–30 are related to Suyu I;

the *acllas* of 30–40 to Suyu II;

the *acllas* of 40–50 to Suyu III; and

the *acllas* of 50–60 to Suyu IV.

Another possible diametrical correspondence between *acllas* and *suyus* involves a model whose existence is also attested elsewhere. The argument is as follows: Huanacauri, although it rises at the horizon of the Temple of the Sun, belongs to the space of the valley, a space that is well delimited and divided into two moieties following a diametrical opposition. We can conclude that there is a correspondence between, on the one hand, the second subdivision—superior to the first and embedded in it—of four age-classes of five years each, and, on the other hand, the subdivision of the valley into two dia-

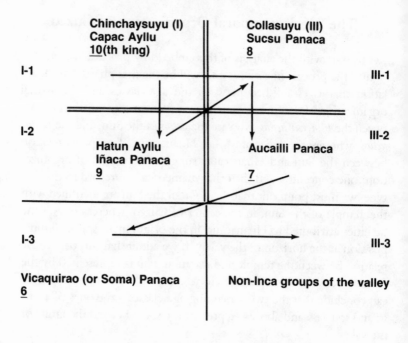

Figure 14. The *panaca* model of Hanan-Cuzco.

metrically opposed moieties and into four *suyus*. Thus the *acllas*
of age 20–25 correspond to Chinchaysuyu (I);
of 30–35 to Collasuyu (II);
of 25–30 to Antisuyu (III);
of 35–40 to Cuntisuyu (IV);
while the whole external space is abandoned to the two last classes,
those of 40–50, and 50–60 and above.

Having reached the second phase of this embedding process, we
have to start all over again, putting in relation the system of age-
classes and the hierarchical and genealogical classification of the *panacas* or noble *ayllus*. We are now dealing with a relation between the
age-class organization and the internal structure of Hanan-Cuzco.
Here the organizational model constituted by Capac Ayllu, the other
four noble *ayllus* recognized as *panacas*, and the sixth group formed
by the non-Inca population of the valley, is rigorously identical to
the age-class model (Figs. 13 and 14).

Let us mention again the characteristics of the prevailing organization in Hanan-Cuzco, that is in the higher moiety of the valley. The five *chapa* districts were hierarchically ranked according to their localization in relation to the city. The *chapas* located upriver generally were superior to the districts located downriver. The king had named as administrators members of his own family and of genealogical ranks corresponding to those of the districts. It is in this privileged relation between the administrator, the district, and its population that I look for the answer to the definition of *panacas*. Now, if we pay attention to the underlined numbers in Figure 14 that indicate the genealogical distance between the king, on the one hand, and his ancestors and the administrators, on the other, we notice that the king and his father belonged to the first *suyu* or quarter (I), while his grandfather and great-grandfather belonged to the other (III), but that his great-great-grandfather belonged to the first *suyu* again, although he occupied a lower position there.

Let us now move on to the names of the *ayllus* and *panacas:* Capac Ayllu is the only noble *ayllu* that is not also recognized as a *panaca*—just as the *aclla* class of *huayrur* is the only one not to bear also the name of *sumac*. In the same way as Vicaquirao Panaca is set apart by the quality of "stinking" attached to it, the fifth age-class of ten years, inasmuch as it is not subdivided into two of five years each, is already suggestive of an inferior status. The non-Inca inhabitants of the valley are assimilated to the *acllas* "of the plain" by the fact that both groups are excluded from their respective organization in the embedding process. Finally, the two *ayllus* Capac and Hatun are opposed to Sucsu and Aucailli in the same way that the lords are opposed to the priests, and that the *acllas* of 20–25 and 25–30, dedicated to the Sun and the major *huacas,* are opposed to the *acllas* of 30–35 and 35–40, devoted to the cult of Huanacauri and the secondary *huacas.* Incidentally, Guaman Poma elsewhere (e.g., p. 280 [282]) gives a list of primary, secondary, and tertiary *huacas,* but this information goes beyond our present purpose.

From the fact that Capac Ayllu (10) *and* Hatun Ayllu (9) correspond, as a group, to the 20–25 and 25–30 age-classes, we can infer that the internal organization of Chinchaysuyu (I) represented a third phase of the embedding process. I have discussed elsewhere

(Zuidema 1964 p. 59 and Ch. 6) the information regarding this phase. Capac Ayllu is at the top of a column made up of three groups: (1) Capac Ayllu; (2) Chavin Cuzco Ayllu, as the non-Inca *ayllu* of Ayar Cachi, brother of Manco Capac in the origin myth; (3) Vicaquirao Panaca. Hatun Ayllu heads the other column, where we find: (1) Hatun Ayllu; (2) Arayraca Ayllu, *ayllu* of the brother Ayar Uchu in the origin myth; (3) the pre-Inca *ayllu* of the Huacaytaqui, "the dancers of the *huacas*."

The diagram of Figure 15 represents the type of hierarchical orga-

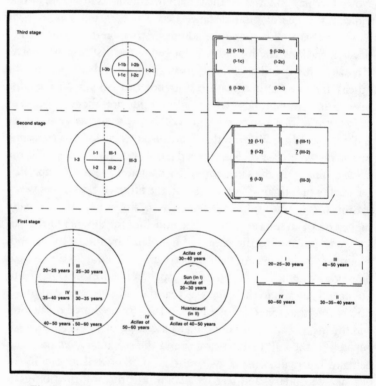

Figure 15. The spatio-temporal organization of Cuzco. By Colin McEwan. (The numbers and letters, in the second and third stages, next to the underlined numbers designating the *panacas*, refer to classifications that will be explained later in connection with the *ceque* system.)

nization produced by the embedding process. There are three stages. Each consists of a concentric phase followed by a diametrical one. The contraction toward the next stage leads to the diametrical representation, but once this is reached, the former stage is represented in a concentric form. The diametrical representation consists of four groups divided into two moieties. But the distribution of these groups changes with the intervention of the hierarchical principle: then the first group belongs to the upper moiety, the second group to the lower moiety, the third, again, to the upper moiety, and the fourth to the lower. There is an alternation. But it is the first moiety which at the next higher stage is again subdivided into four groups. The formalization of the embedding process permits a finer analysis of the spatio-temporal organization of the Cuzco Valley, an analysis which leads us to the calendrical organization.

Coming to a provisional conclusion, I will recall the production of textiles—a rich topic which should allow us to bring together data that to this point we had only considered in relative isolation from one another: age-classes, *panacas,* and mythology. I took as point of departure for my analysis the study of the *chapa* districts which, as local units, allowed their lords the possibility of being represented at the Court on various social and ritual occasions. Through the use of certain kinship terms such as *concha,* "nephew," these cognatic descendants, these "princes of the blood," could be represented as if they were members of various matrilines connected at different genealogical levels to the royal patriline. But the field of application of the word *panaca* also assigned to these groups of relatives a representative role during the rites connected with the age-classes. Later on I will offer an example from which it will become clear that, because of its mediatory quality, such a role bridges over to the third function of the *panacas:* their calendrical function. For it was in fact the *panacas* who assumed the celebration of the monthly rites. We will then observe of the *panacas* that they acted ritually at distinct hierarchical levels by means of different temporal levels embedded one into another.

We have seen the close relation between the last three age-classes— more specifically the fourth and fifth—and textile production. We could suggest a comparison with the *panacas* of Antisuyu (III), recalling the fact that the eponymous god Viracocha (Taylor Ch. 1), the king Viracocha Inca (no. 8) (Sarmiento Ch. 25), and Tupa Amaru Inca (Santacruz Pachacuti p. 242) were regarded as the inventors of textiles of the *tucapu* type: cloths decorated with *tucapu* signs. Guaman Poma represents the dress of Viracocha Inca with the full field emblazoned with *tucapu* signs, and that of Yahuar Huacac, ancestor of the seventh *panaca*, with only the half-field emblazoned. This comparison between the age-classes of the weaver *acllas* and the *panacas* of the kings numbered eight and seven would constitute an excellent introduction to a more advanced study of the rich material contained in Guaman Poma's drawings illustrating his chronicle, where are depicted in great detail the dress of kings and queens and of all the civil servants who, through the operation of genealogical groups and age-classes, are integrated into the administrative and ritual system that I am analyzing here.

◁ 5 ▷

The Provincial Organization of 40,000 Families and the Calendar of 328 Days

Having set for myself the task of interpreting the spatio-temporal organization in Cuzco, I have mentioned on several occasions the Incas-by-privilege. In my analysis of the origin myth, I remarked that the grandparents of Manco Capac belonged to the two pre-Inca capitals óf Maras and Sutic, located in the territory of the Incas-by-privilege. I then analyzed the information given by Betanzos on the ten *chapa* districts and on the services owed the Inca king by the ten lords of these Incas-by-privilege and their people: services that consisted principally in the canalization of the Cuzco Valley. Guaman Poma assigns these lords, by way of the four *suyus,* to a sixth genealogical category, inferior to that of great-great-grandchildren and *huaccha concha.* This allows us to rank them at the same genealogical level as the *cacacuzco,* the "brothers of non-related wives," natives of the valley itself. In all these examples the element of time played an important role. It is this element that I want to bring to the fore, still within the frame of an interest in the Incas-by-privilege, by returning to the Incaic notion of "province," called *huamani* (Santillán p. 47) according to the number of families (40,000) it was supposed to contain.

An anonymous source relates how in Cuzco, for the ritual opening of the agricultural season, the first person to plow was the Inca king, followed by the lords of the four *suyus,* territories determined in function of their capacity to support 100,000 families; then came the forty lords who each controlled political units 10,000 families strong (Rostworowski 1970 pp. 164–166). The anonymous author does not hesitate to extend this model of the forty lords to the organization of the whole empire. (For a similar notion of ten provinces in the Inca Empire, see *Relación de las costumbres antiguas de los naturales del Pirú,* pp. 154–155.) Other sources suggest the application of a similar model, but based on forty lords each heading 1,000 families, to a provincial organization of 40,000 families. Cuzco was the typical example for this model of an organization that included the city itself, the valley, and the Incas-by-privilege. The fact that the latter were regularly summoned to Cuzco to plow and harvest attests their importance, not only in economic matters, but even more cogently in the ritual and religious domains. Their presence was required to prepare the earth to receive the seed by plowing and irrigating; to make "Mother Earth" fertile by sowing; to facilitate the growth and ripening of the plants; and finally to assure the harvest.

The first chronicler to have experience with such a system, as outlined here, but then also in its temporal aspect and as related to female organization, was Pedro Pizarro (pp. 47, 65–66), one of the conquerors who befriended Atahuallpa, the last Inca king, when he was in prison in Cajamarca.[32] Drawing on his personal experience with Atahuallpa, he claims that the king took his "sisters" as wives, one "lineage" of these belonging to the "line" of the king himself. Pizarro, then, distinguishes between the queen as sister and other sisters. Moreover, the king had "all the daughters of the lords in his kingdom as concubines, serving his principal sisters, and those [concubines] were more than four thousand." Each of the principal sisters was with the king in turn for a week of eight days. A rather late source (P. Herrera p. 88) in Quito specifies this tradition about Atahuallpa, observing that the king, in addition to the queen, called on the services of forty wives or sisters.[33] As other data, to be mentioned presently, indicate that each sister was served by one hundred concubines, we might suggest that such a system of $1 + 40 = 41$ "sisters" already was underlying Pizarro's report and that it corresponded to a calendar of so many weeks.[34] Pizarro, moreover, already used the term "sister" in the sense of the "sisters" of the king in Cuzco from whom descended the *panacas*, the groups descending from his secondary wives as "sisters," and to which belonged the secondary children called *concha*, "sister's child."

Guaman Poma (pp. 453–457 [455–459]) and Martín de Murúa (Bk. 2, Ch. 13) allow us to reconstruct a system, similar to that of Pizarro, of alliances between the Incas in Cuzco and the forty lords of the Incas-by-privilege. The king in Cuzco gave in marriage to lords of provinces of 40,000, 20,000, 10,000 or 5,000 families either his sisters, his kinswomen, or other women of high lineage. Lords of 1,000 families received noble ladies or *acllas* native to their own provinces. Although their marriages were concluded in the presence of the king and in Cuzco, it was the provincial overlords of 10,000 families who actually gave them their wives. These ladies, attached to groups of 1,000 families, were called *iñaca* (Guaman Poma p. 760[774]).

Both authors, but especially Murúa, provide us with elaborate lists of sumptuary laws promulgated for the occasion and of the presents bestowed on these lords according to their rank. Among these presents figure "100 to 150 maids who came from the *storehouses* [i.e., the houses of *acllas* or "chosen women"], or else had been captured during the war." Murúa is referring here to the *paco acllas* mentioned by Bertonio, and to a type of female services to which Pedro Pizarro already had drawn our attention. The idea of the 100 maids is one that recurs in various other forms in the descriptions of the Inca dynasty; in those of the *panaca* organization; and in the ritual calendar that, in Cuzco, governed agricultural tasks. This point urges us to study in more detail the distribution of the *iñaca* ladies given in marriage to the forty lords of 1,000 families, the "ladies-in-waiting" who served the queen as "sisters" and who were the secondary wives of the king. We are dealing with a spatial and temporal organization interpreted in terms of the calendar which ordered the individual lifetime according to astral observations. The data about the calendar and the tallying of the days of the year constitute the logical outcome of the system of relations that I have been able to establish between time and space. I will conclude my study by analyzing the integration of the category of *iñaca* ladies into the so-called *ceque* system and the calendar represented by it.

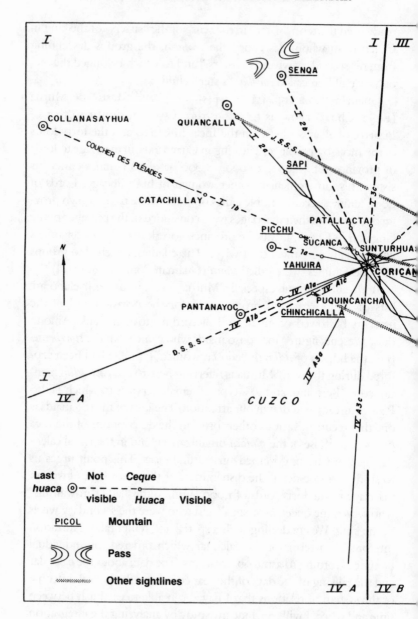

Figure 16. The *ceques* used for astronomical observations.

D.S.S.R.: Sunrise at the December solstice. D.S.S.S.: Sunset at the December solstice. J.S.S.S.: Sunset at the June solstice. Z.S.R.: Sunrise during the two passages of the sun through zenith. A.Z.S.S.: Sunset in the opposite

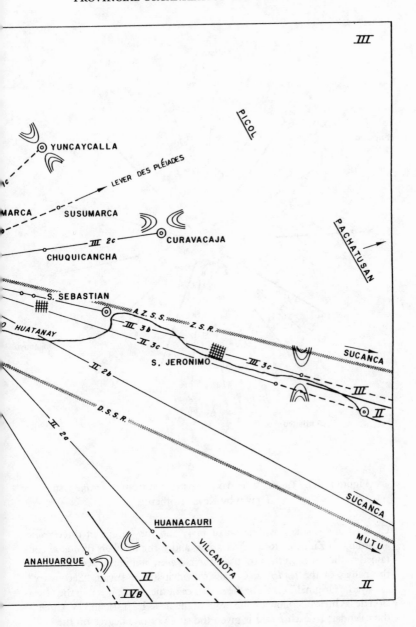

(antizenith) direction, six months after the two zenith sunrises. *Ceques* III-2b and I-1b: rise and set of the Pleiades. *Ceques* IVB-3b and IVA-3a: rise and set of the Southern Cross and of the stars α and β Centaurus.

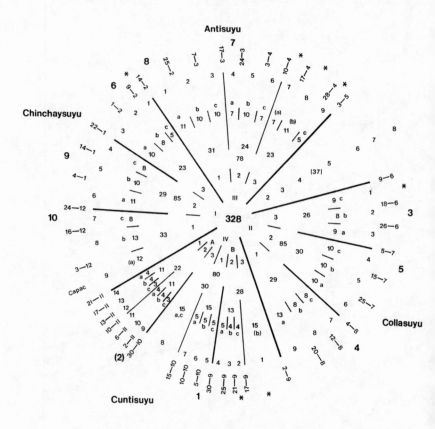

Figure 17. The 328-day calendar reconstructed from the *ceque* system.
Drawn by Kevin Rotheroe.

Circles 1 and 2: the classification of *suyus* and the groups of three *ceques* according to Zuidema 1964. Circles 3, 4, and 5: the numbers of *huacas* contained in the *suyus;* in the groups of three *ceques;* and in the *ceques*. Circle 5: the names of the *ceques:* a, Collana, "Principal"; b, Payan, "Secondary"; c, Cayao, "Original." Circle 6: the sequence of the *ceques,* given in the "Relación de las huacas" following the order of the *suyus* I, III, II, and IV. Circle 7: the calendar; to each *huaca* is given the space of one degree on the circle, each degree corresponding to one day. Circle 8: the numbers and asterisks; *panacas* and pre-Inca *ayllus* mentioned in the "Relación de las huacas."

The interest that the Incas took in the territory of the valley and in the surrounding lands, as sources of fertility and fecundity, led them to create for themselves a geographical representation of the country through a system of forty-one directions or vectors—the *ceques*—radiating toward various points on the horizon (Cobo Bk. 13, Ch. 5, p. 158; Chs. 13–16, pp. 169–186; Rowe 1979; Zuidema 1977b). This system permitted the location of 328 sacred places: mostly springs, mountains, or hills. Each sacred place or *huaca* was the object of a special cult on an assigned day, according to a succession established by the ranking of the *ceques* which followed a descending hierarchical order: series of the *suyus* (I, II, III, and IV); groups of three *ceques* (1, 2, and 3), and individual *ceques* (a, b, and c). Suyu IV itself was divided in two *sub-suyus*, IVA and IVB, each with three groups of *ceques*; IVA-3 only had two *ceques*, a and c, and they were perceived as forming only one; IVB-3 only had one *ceque*, b. The highest-ranking *ceque*, IV-1a, was called *capac*, "royal."

The *ceque* system fulfilled two distinct functions: the first consisted in the delimitation of space, and certain *ceques* played an important part in the codification of astronomical observations (Fig. 16). The other function had to do with using the system somewhat like a rosary, to order the *huacas* according to the days of the year. The 328 *huacas* integrated in the *ceque* system were not distributed regularly, as could have been expected, at the rate of 8 *huacas* on each of the 41 *ceques*. This, among other reasons, was because the *huacas* of a *ceque* or a group of *ceques* were used in the measurement of the days between distinct astronomical observations, those of the Sun, the stars, or the Moon (Fig. 17).

Each *panaca* was associated with one of the groups of three *ceques*, and I have represented in Figure 17 these relations as given by Cobo (see also Fig. 11). For each *huaca* I have left an interval of 1 degree (of a circle that, ideally, has 365 degrees) representing one day, and the dates registered between the periods defined by the *ceques* mark the amount of time lapsed. The responsibility in Cuzco for the celebration of rituals according to their calendrical relevance fell on the *panacas* and on some of the other *ayllus* (Zuidema 1982b; 1982c; 1983). In addition, we can consider that each of the forty *ceques*, excluding the very first of the system, called *capac*, was connected to one of the groups of Incas-by-privilege defined as groups of 1,000 families, and that each *ceque* would have been likely to be spatially oriented in the direction where that group lived. Finally, we find that there must have existed two discrete systems that accounted for the division of the 328 days into 41 time-units: a regular system consisting of 41 "weeks" of 8 days; and another, irregular one, that totalized in days the real time lapsed between two astronomical observations entered in the calendar. This latter system also took into account the relative social ranking of the *panacas*, of the *ayllus*, and of the groups of Incas-by-privilege.[35]

I do not need to go any further into the intricacies of the *ceque* system to carry on with my analysis of the category of *iñaca* ladies married to the lords of 1,000 families. It will suffice to examine more closely the groups of *ceques* ranked sixth, the lowest rankings in both Hanan-Cuzco and Hurin-Cuzco. Not associated with any of the ten *panacas*, but in an exclusive relation with the autochthonous non-Inca population living in the valley, these two groups of *ceques* (III-3 in Hanan-Cuzco, and IV-3, divided into IVA-3a, c and IVB-3b in Hurin-Cuzco) occupied a central position in the system, different from that of the other groups; a position attested essentially by their technical use as temporal and spatial markers (Zuidema 1985b; in press d). The two functions of the system—to define space on land and in the sky, and to register in calendrical time the interval between two astronomical observations—were quite distinct, and we should not expect that for each of the forty-one *ceques* a direct correspondence could be determined between the two functions. However, the Incas themselves established such a correspondence in regard to the *ceques* of III-3 and IV-3, two cases where astronomical observation conducted along these *ceques* was entered into the calendar by way of exactly the same *ceques*.

In April, the orientation of the *ceques* of III-3 was used in the centripetal direction toward Cuzco to observe the setting of the Sun, an observation that was conducted at the time when the star was going through the nadir, half a year after it had reached its zenith (Zuidema 1981). In the same month of April, there was a tallying of the *huacas* of these *ceques,* and rituals were celebrated that sanctioned the results of the observation, for it was in this direction—along the axis of these *ceques*—that the harvest in procession was brought into Cuzco. Let us recall that, according to the origin myth, Mama Huaco, one of Manco Capac's sisters, was supposed to have entered the city from the very same direction. The procession was conducted in honor of Mama Huaco, who had given the Incas their first seeds, and she was worshipped as a goddess of corn (Molina "el Cuzqueño" 1943 pp. 66–67; Hernández Príncipe p. 466; Zuidema 1977–1978).

The directions IVA-3a, c, and IVB-3b served respectively in the observation of the setting and rising of the brightest stars close to the south celestial pole—i.e., the Southern Cross and the stars α and β of the constellation Centaurus—by way of which the southern direction could be determined (Zuidema and Urton; Zuidema 1982b). The Incas conducted this observation during the only two months of the year when, at the latitude of Cuzco, these stars disappeared below the horizon during part of the night, so that the two phenomena (the setting and the rising) could be observed in the same night. In the *ceque* calendar, this period—from 2 September to 30 October—was counted out in *huacas,* starting with the ones in IVB-3b and finishing with those located in IVA-3a, c. September was the first month of sowing; the month dedicated to the queen, when women were allowed to invite men; when the ritual expulsion from the city of all evils and illnesses took place, in all the directions determined by the *ceques*. Finally, it was the month when dissent between inhabitants of the city was not tolerated (Molina "el Cuzqueño" 1943 pp. 29–32; Zuidema 1964; 1982c; 1989c). During that time, when seeds germinated, the priests of the Sun, the Tarpuntay—from *tarpuy,* "to plant"—fasted and abstained from all sexual contact, subjecting themselves to this regimen of abstinence until the young shoots reached one finger in height, that is to say during the whole two months when Pachamama—the "Earth-Mother"—was in gestation.[36]

We are dealing here with two female deities: the first one, Mama Huaco, is associated with the direction of the *ceques* of III-3 as ancestral deity of the Inca conquerors who came out of the cave of Pacaritambo, south of Cuzco. The second deity, Pachamama, is associated with the *ceques* of IV-3, oriented due south in the direction of the very same cave from which the Inca people emerged. The relation between her and Mama Huaco is included in the account by Santacruz Pachacuti Yamqui where he opposes Manco Capac and his brothers and sisters (including Mama Huaco) to the house of his father, Apu Tambo, "Lord House," and mother, Pachamama Achi, "Earth-Mother-Diviner" (Fig. 2). The *ceques* of IV-3 due south were also associated with the female ancestral deity of the autochthonous population of the Cuzco Valley itself. It is more specifically in reference to the direction IVB-3b that we can bring together the ritual and mythological data that explain the importance given by the Incas to their alliance with the Incas-by-privilege, as source of fecundity and prosperity.

The *ceque* IVB-3b was pointed toward a mountain, Anahuarque, which was an object of worship for the autochthonous population of the valley. It was the only mountain to have risen with the waters of the Flood, and, in honor of its "rise" in those faraway times, boys celebrated during their initiation a fertility ritual that consisted in following down the mountain the girls that had been assigned to them as partners (Molina "el Cuzqueño" 1943 p. 54). For the autochthonous people Mama Anahuarque was their "grandmother and aunt" (probably a father's father's sister), while the Inca conquerors called these descendants of "Mother Anahuarque" the *cacacuzco*, the "male relatives of a non-related wife" (Rostworowski 1962 pp. 137, 154–155). However, we find Mama Anahuarque also represented as an Inca queen, and as such the administrative system transformed her into the ancestral representative of the *iñaca* ladies married to lords of 1,000 families. From this we can conclude that she evoked at the same time Mount Anahuarque, the *ceque* called Anahuarque that leads to it, and the period of the year defined by this *ceque*.

There exist several versions of the myth of Queen Mama Anahuarque, but there is a certain consensus to see in her the queen of Pachacuti Inca, the ninth king. The characteristics that are always mentioned in connection with her are either her own prodigious fecundity—she is said to have given birth to 150 children, of whom 100 were sons and 50 were daughters—or the 150 illegitimate children her husband had; or else the 100 or 150 maids who waited on her (e.g., Betanzos Part 1, Ch. 17; Sarmiento Ch. 47; Murúa Bk. 2, Ch. 13). This is the reason why her husband's *panaca* is called Hatun

Ayllu, the large *ayllu*," and also Iñaca Panaca, the *panaca* of the men born of *iñaca* women.[37] We remember that, while Guaman Poma had nothing to say about the organization of the *panacas* and *ayllus* in Cuzco, he refers to the word *iñaca* as a title belonging to the ladies of Incas-by-privilege in Cuntisuyu (IV) (see Fig. 5).[38] In terms of the *ceque* system, this way of ranking can be formulated as follows: the sixth group of three *ceques* (IVA-3a, c and IVB-3b) in Hurin-Cuzco is associated with the autochthonous population of the valley and is represented by Mama Anahuarque as the mythical ancestress of the *cacacuzco*. From her association with *iñaca* ladies we can conclude that Guaman Poma assigns to these ladies, belonging to groups of 1,000 families, the same kind of rank.

Murúa specifies that the 100 or 150 maids were *acllas*—those called *paco acllas* by Bertonio—women chosen to contribute to the proper functioning of the state, and who, rising through the age-class system, could reach the Court of the Inca. In fact, the queen herself and the ladies of high lineage figured at the top of that female hierarchy. All of them were part of the redistributive system through which women offered to the king as wives were shared by him among the people he wished to honor. Pizarro (p. 47) and Sarmiento (Ch. 47) claim that all women of the Inca Empire belonged by right to the monarch as "sisters" and wives, a right that enabled him to redistribute them to their future husbands. Such a right allows us to conclude that the wives or secondary "sisters," possibly numbering forty, who in succession were ladies of honor at the Court probably were none other than the ladies of the Incas-by-privilege.[39] Just like their husbands, they were obliged to appear regularly at the Court of the Inca king and queen. Their husbands' presence was required during plowing and perhaps also at other times. The wives served for about eight days each, but the exact number of days may have varied depending on their rank and the place that they occupied in the calendar. The myth of Yahuar Huacac had presented us with a system of symmetric marriage exchange between himself, king of the Incas in Cuzco, and Topay Capac, king of the Ayarmacas in Maras—a type of marriage that was equidistant from that of his father, who still owed allegiance to a pre-Inca king, and that of his son, whose kingdom already comprised a group of Incas-by-privilege. In the myth of

Pachacuti Inca this system developed into one of a redistribution of women. His own marriage became the prototype of the system of *panacas,* the groups descending from "sisters" which organized the children of the king called *concha,* "sisters' children." We now see how, and this will be my provisional conclusion, the Inca kinship system, which combines a strongly hierarchized social organization with a pattern of symmetrical marriage exchanges, presents us with an elaborate notion of the redistributive principle, applied not only to women, but also to land, goods, privileges, or even ideas: a principle whose action cogently pervades all levels of cultural life.[40]

◄ Conclusion ►

I have attempted here to construct a model operatively valid at several levels: namely, of two moieties, each consisting of six ranked groups. The different representations of an identical structure permit a better understanding of the model itself. I took as a starting point of this work two social facts that, thanks to trustworthy colonial documentation, can be studied thoroughly—although our study clearly has not yet exhausted their wealth of information.

The first of these two facts deals with the existence and the delimitation of the *chapas* as irrigation districts. It is possible to do a topographical survey of the rivers in a given district and of the corresponding irrigation canals. We can document such networks from an archaeological perspective (Niles 1987). In places where the descendants of the Incas and their villages have disappeared, there remain the political groups which have taken their place and which continue to use the same canalization networks (Sherbondy 1982a; Zuidema in press a).

The second fact that I selected as object of analysis has to do with the Incas-by-privilege and their descendants in colonial times. This analysis derived from my reading of the origin myth; this central theme concerned sociopolitical and economic relations, as well as ritual and marriage alliances between Cuzco and the surrounding area. The internal organization of each group of Incas-by-privilege probably reproduced that of Cuzco and its valley. It is still possible to study archaeologically[41] and ethnographically[42] the enduring traces of the ceremonial relations that existed between Cuzco, the *panacas* and *ayllus* of its valley, and the Incas-by-privilege. Thus, for instance, till recently the road from Pacaritambo to Cuzco was still maintained by men from Pacaritambo; it was divided into sections according to the number of *ayllus* of the village, each *ayllu* being responsible for its own section of the road (Urton 1984 pp. 36–37). People from towns and villages around Cuzco live in the city, one of their stated purposes being to represent here the interests of their places of origin. This is the same type of representation as the one of ten *chapas*, mentioned by Betanzos, related to the ten irrigation districts in the Cuzco Valley. The political groups called upon to appear at the Court could claim rights of usufruct of the lands that had been allocated to them.

We know of similar cases concerning Inca regional capitals, such as Vilcas Huaman, which the Spanish conquerors, passing through the place on their march to Cuzco, found totally deserted. The Spanish presence at Cajamarca had been enough for the non-autochthonous population of Vilcas Huaman to abandon the city, where they had been living mostly as representatives of the surrounding villages. For this reason, it seems to me quite likely that at the time of the Conquest, in Cuzco itself and its valley, the native pre-Inca population would have been a minority, and even that a large majority of the Inca population proper had already abandoned it in the very first days of the Conquest. This is why I have—I believe, successfully— confronted the dual problem of the demographic question in Cuzco and of the hierarchical breakdown of its population, by studying first the demographic structure of the whole region, including the Incas-by-privilege, for whom we have demographic and statistical data more reliable than for Cuzco itself (Cook; Zuidema and Poole).

Besides the problem of the *chapas* and of the Incas-by-privilege, I was able to study the Inca administrative system of the valley and the Cuzco region, from the hierarchical and genealogical composition of the king's family. The rank of an administrator corresponded to the rank of the group he administered, in proportion to the size of its territory, its distance from Cuzco, the hierarchical position of the group in its own locality, and various other factors. At first, I left aside the concept of *panaca,* as it was presented to us by the later chroniclers and uncritically accepted in the modern scientific and popular literature. These chroniclers claim that each king founded his own *panaca,* made up of all his descendants with the exception of the heir to the throne. According to this version of Inca history, the *panaca* would simply be the genealogical group liable to claim new lands. Furthermore—still according to this version—after the death of the king, his properties, movable and immovable, were exclusively dedicated to the maintenance of his cult. Arguing from this fact, the American archaeologist G. W. Conrad (1981)[43] recently tried to give a causal explanation of the great conquests of the Incas. All the possessions of the dead monarch would have been exclusively reserved for the cult of his mummy, while his son in turn would have been forced to gather his own riches. This hypothesis leads to postulating a number of propositions that are difficult to uphold and that nothing in the main chronicles seems to support.

If we believe in a historical formation of the *panacas,* the fact that there were exactly ten *panacas* in the Cuzco Valley, and only ten, loses all interpretative value. In fact, the information that I have used here attests to the existence, in Cuzco, of an organization within which one unique model functioned at different social and ritual levels. Thus I have been able to clearly establish the relations between the internal organization of the royal family and the territorial organization connected with the irrigation districts. By presenting the organization of the royal family as a manifestation of the process of attributing titles and administrative functions, I have succeeded in integrating some very rich and complex material. In addition, I have been able, for the benefit of further research, to touch upon the study of the relation between the administrators and the social group or the territory they administered. The data concerning Tupa Amaru suggest, for instance, that the "lands of Amaru" were a territory assigned to an administrative function, and not an inheritance transmitted in a genealogical line.

In the mythic and ritual information concerning the ancestor-kings, the *panacas,* the calendric rites, the *ceques,* and the *huacas,* information that also includes material on gods, ritual dress, and other such elements, we can see a symbolic language, in itself a coherent whole, comparable for the wealth of its data to any of the Mexican codices, whether prehispanic or colonial. If those Mexican documents are richer from the artistic point of view, in turn, the *ceque* system and the other material featured in our Peruvian "codex" allow a better reincorporation of the data in a global representation of the society.

To order the mass of available data on Cuzco, I first had to analyze a series of rather complex pieces of information. For that reason I will offer in conclusion a simplified model of the organization of the city, taking into account however all the essential elements.

The Inca genealogical model consisted of six generations: that of the king, those of the four ancestors, and the generation to which belonged the autochthonous pre- and non-Inca population of the Cuzco Valley. The sons and daughters of women situated at comparable genealogical and hierarchical levels, but of non-Inca origin and foreign to Cuzco, formed a parallel organization to the first one, so that the two organizations presented themselves as a whole divided into two halves.

According to the Inca genealogical doctrine, there was only one "straight" line endowed with a patrilineal type organization: that of the kings and queens, themselves sisters of the kings, born of the same fathers and mothers. In relation to the members of this straight line, all the children who were not heirs to the throne were called "sister's children" and grouped into *ayllu* types of organization that integrated not only these other descendants of a common ancestor, but also those of the ancestor's sister. Considering the structure from the political angle, we note that Cuzco was divided into four administrative units or *suyus*. The royal family—*ayllu*—belonged to Suyu I (Chinchaysuyu), which comprised the city itself and all its springs and sources of water; the members of that *ayllu* were represented within this Suyu I, at all its hierarchical and genealogical levels. As for the other three *suyus*, they possessed a comparable internal organization, but in addition were placed under the control of administrators mandated by the central government, that is to say that they were accountable to Suyu I. It is the coexistence of these two types of administration, one internal and the other externally controlled, which misled the Spaniards in regard to the organization of the Cuzco Valley. The model that I suggest here is very close to the one we know well through some seventeenth-century documents for Central Peru (Duviols 1986; Zuidema 1973a; 1977–1978), a region where the chroniclers were not so mystified, as in the case of Cuzco, by Inca imperial history and the ceremonial superstructure.

◄ Notes ►

1. I will spell words and names in Quechua, the language of the Incas, as found in the original sources and as is traditional in Peru.

2. Nonetheless, the studies of Duviols (1966), Taylor (1987), A. Acosta (1987), and Salomon (n.d.) make us aware that the Huarochiri manuscript of Francisco de Ávila, written at least fifty years after the Conquest, also was a reaction to its own times.

3. For a presentation and study of all the relevant versions of these myths, see Urbano 1981.

4. Murra 1980 (1956); 1975. An excellent overview of his work and of the studies that it generated is given in Masuda, Shimada, and Morris, eds. 1985.

5. These "months" do not cover, however, the whole period of the tropical year, but only one of 328 days, of importance for agriculture. I will not deal here with the extra thirteenth period (see Zuidema 1988).

6. For a more detailed description of the peoples who lived in the province of the Incas-by-privilege, see Rowe 1946 pp. 184–191; Zuidema 1983; 1985b; and Zuidema and Poole 1982.

7. Guaman Poma (p. 150), in fact, mentions Acos as the southern pre-Inca capital, but on the basis of the parallel to Maras as the northern capital (Guaman Poma p. 97), I suspect that in Santacruz Pachacuti's version of the origin myth Sutic replaces Acos.

8. The length of the valley from the city to Chapa 3 was about 20 kilometers. For the location of Chapas 10 to 6, the work of Sherbondy (1982a) was especially helpful, although in recent fieldwork I came to some different results (Zuidema in press a). For Chapas 5 to 1, other documents and ethnographic research were used.

9. Betanzos is the only chronicler who uses the concept of *chapa*, but the

word and its derivatives were well known in the sixteenth century and are mentioned in all the Quechua and Aymara dictionaries. For Santo Tomás, in 1560, *chapa* or *chacara* is "a piece of arable land"; *chapac* or *yayanc* (from *yaya*, "father") means "landowner" and *chapay*, "jurisdiction." *Chapacuni* and *sayuacuni* (from *sayua*, "marker") mean "to inherit"; and *sayuani* and *cequeni*, "to delimit a piece of land." The dictionary edited by Ricardo in 1584 mentions *chapaquey* "used by Indians for the Spanish encomendero"; González Holguín, writing in 1608, is more explicit. Among other applications he mentions *chacracta chapacuni*, "to pick and choose before anybody else in the repartition of communal lands," and *chapaqquey*, "my encomendero who takes possession of me as if I were something to be taken instead of a free man." In a similar way, *chapac* is used in the mythology of Huarochiri for the first person to conquer lands and appropriate them (Taylor 1987 Ch. 24, p. 371). Bertonio, in 1612, adds that in Aymara *chapallitha* means "to throw lumps or clods of earth (on the ridges) during plowing; it is the work of women" and *chapaca* or *sapaca* means "sperm" and "tree roots." In the verb *chapallitha* we find the root *chapa* as a concept similar to that of *chuta*, studied by Urton (1984), and also of *ceque*, a word that I personally heard used in Ayacucho to designate "furrow," and for which Santo Tomás gives the meaning of "delimited land." Wachtel (1980–1981) analyzed the words *urco* and *suyu*, used to designate pieces of land similar in form to furrows allocated by the Inca administration in the valley of Cochabamba, Bolivia, to the *mitimaes*, populations "displaced" by order of the administration. However Molina "el Cuzqueño" (1943 pp. 31–32) applies the term *mitima* to Incas-by-privilege who lived around Cuzco—people who were not in the least "displaced," but to whom *chapas* had been granted in exchange for the services that they all had to provide following a system of rotation (*mita*) in the Cuzco Valley. (See Mannheim 1986 on the relation between the words *mita* and *mitmac*.) Finally, I would like to stress the dual meaning of the word *ceque*, which designates (1) the strips of land or parallel furrows, a meaning that is close to that of *chapa*, *chuta*, *urco*, and *suyu*; and (2) the forty-one directions, radiating from the Temple of the Sun to the horizon, in the Cuzco Valley.

10. For the modern use of the term *ayllu*, where the same kinds of distinctions are made, see B. J. Isbell 1977; 1978 Ch. 5.

11. See also Zuidema 1964 pp. 123–126.

12. At the same time the article was written, other authors stressed the properties of the *ayllu* as a kindred: see Bolton and Mayer, eds. 1977 and also Mayer and Bolton, eds. 1980, where more articles are included. Excellent overviews of these and later studies are given by Ossio (1980; 1983). How-

ever, only one later author, Abercrombie (1986), pays attention in terms of ethnographic experience to the problem that is central to my argument: the equation of mother's brother to wife's father.

13. Through personal information of Professor Frank Salomon which I gratefully recognize here. The model is found in Martyr Coma 1574, p. 95.

14. The problem relates also to that of *compadrazgo* as it is applied in modern Andean culture (Ossio 1984).

15. The description is found in one of the myths from Huarochiri (Taylor Ch. 8, p. 151), where it is given as additional information to clarify the argument of the myth.

16. According to Taylor, the two names of the first sister should be read as Paltacha and Cochucha (Ch. 8) or Cotucha (Ch. 13), and the name of the second sister as Cobapacha (Ch. 8) or Copacha (Ch. 13), which readings are somewhat different from those in earlier editions. In the French edition of this book (published in 1986) I had tentatively interpreted the reading Poltacha for the first sister as meaning "queen," comparing it to a name Pocacha given by Betanzos (1968) for "queen" in Cuzco. But this name also turns out to be a misreading for Paxxa (= *pacsa*, "full moon") (Betanzos 1987). In an early (1551) account of Inca government and nobility (Rowe 1966 p. 38), a term *paxia* is mentioned for "principal lady." If we are allowed to read this term as *paxxa* = *pacsa*, it confirms Betanzos' statement and the term might possibly be approached to that of *paltacha* in Huarochiri as a misspelling of *pacsa-cha*. A local informant from San Damián told Taylor in 1980 that the name Cotucha is a local toponym, of interest for the old myths in which it occurs (Taylor Ch. 13, p. 227; Ch. 31, p. 475).

17. On earlier occasions I have called the "noble" *ayllus* "royal" *ayllus*. I defer from doing so now in order to distinguish the *panacas* from Capac Ayllu as the only true "Royal Ayllu."

18. This point is made especially clear in the myth (Taylor Ch. 8, p. 17) where the names of the twelve "brothers" and "sisters" are given (see Fig. 9). The god Pariacaca fights in the form of five brothers against an enemy whom he adopts as a sixth, albeit "stinking," "brother" after defeating him.

19. For the calendrical significance of the myth; see Chapter 5.

20. Bertonio mentions the ritual under the name of *sucullu*. For a discussion see Zuidema 1989c. Avila mentions the ritual in his first appendix to the mythology of Huarochiri (Taylor pp. 488–511).

21. Dumézil (1973) analyzed the theme of Mater Matuta, that of two mothers, in the mythology of India and in Roman rituals. In the first case, the Sun God had Night as his first mother and Dawn as his second.

22. For a first reference to this type of royal succession, see Zárate (1555)

1968 Ch. 13, pp. 53–54, in the unexpurgated edition of his chronicle from before 1577 (Duviols 1964; see also Bataillon 1960; 1963–1964).

23. Sarmiento, writing 19 years later, must have read Betanzos' chronicle and elaborated upon it. He added 5 years to the age of Pachacuti, making him die at 125, and then assigned to all former kings similar ages, whereas Betanzos hardly was interested in their persons at all and did not mention their ages. According to Sarmiento, Pachacuti Inca died in 1191. Tupa Yupanqui "only" reigned for 67 years and Huayna Capac for 60; the first died in the year 1258 and the second in the year 1524 (having ascended to the throne in 1464) (Zuidema 1964 pp. 232–235). Betanzos used Pachacuti Inca's age as a device to include more generations after him. But Sarmiento, by giving the whole dynasty such a mythical length, left a lapse of 206 years open between the reigns of Pachacuti Inca and Huayna Capac. Either device suggests that there was more than one generation between Pachacuti Inca and Huayna Capac.

24. Garcilaso does this in a context where one would not have expected such a statement: that of the urban planning of Cuzco.

25. This section on Inca history was rewritten and expanded after the new and complete version of the chronicle of Betanzos became known in 1987. Shortly before this date, Rowe (1985) had reconstructed a model of eight *panacas* as it might have been instituted by Pachacuti Inca, later to be changed by Huayna Capac. There are different reasons to argue that such a reconstruction is not valid. First of all, not only Betanzos, but other chroniclers as well, clearly indicate that Pachacuti Inca instituted not eight *panacas* but ten. Rowe's argument is that, as Pachacuti Inca was the ninth king, this king needed an organization of eight *panacas* to account for his ancestors. For the same reason, he claims, Huayna Capac, the eleventh king, would have changed the primitive organization into one of ten *panacas*. Rowe, on the one hand, accepts the idea that the organization of *panacas* followed a regular model and that there was a certain detachment between the *panaca* model and the dynastic sequence. It is for that reason that he assumes that Tupa Yupanqui, the tenth king, could not have changed the organization, as in his time there would have been five kings in Hurin and four in Hanan. Nonetheless, he wants to maintain their historical sequence and feels forced to redistribute the "original" eight *panacas* over the four *suyus* or quarters of Cuzco, with two *panacas* to each *suyu*. Thus he wants to regain a balance between them. This seems to me an inadmissable procedure and without any foundation in the facts. Anyhow, the question as asked by Rowe now is largely academic and is settled by Betanzos: all ten *panacas* originated after Pachacuti Inca, and their number was not dependent on the number of former kings.

26. From a formal point of view, this Andean organization offers remarkable similarities with the age-class structures of the Ge cultures in Brasil (e.g., Nimuendajú 1946; Maybury-Lewis 1967) as well as with those of the northwestern Amazonian cultures studied by Christine Hugh-Jones (1979), Stephen Hugh-Jones (1979), and Patrice Bidou (1976). In this particular instance, the comparative analysis could be productive to help us to understand the real functioning of the age-classes in Cuzco and their possible relation to the *panacas* in the calendar. With the study of age-classes, we are then provided with yet another possibility to consider Andean culture in the wider context of South American Indian cultures.

27. This was told to me during fieldwork in the Río Pampas area, Department of Ayacucho.

28. See also Alberti Manzanares 1985; 1986; 1987.

29. But information of Betanzos (1987 Bk. 1, Ch. 17) and later chroniclers might also be interpreted thus. See Chapter 5 here.

30. For a recent discussion of the concept of "beauty" in Andean culture, including the beauty of *acllas* and especially those called *huayrur,* see Cereceda 1987. The author also discusses the relation between this term and *huayruru.* The identity of the two terms in their use for *acllas* is clear from Calancha (p. 1147), who uses *guayruru* for the *acllas.*

31. Molina "el Cuzqueño" (1943 p. 34; see also p. 49) mentions how at one moment during the planting rituals of the Situa in the month of Coyaraymi, the "Feast of the Queen" in September, a woman also came out, called Coya Pacsa, "Queen Moon," as wife of the Sun, who was a sister or daughter of the reigning king. See also Cobo (Bk. 13, Ch. 37).

32. Pizarro, however, did not write about his experiences then until 1571. I am using the edition (1978) based on the manuscript of the Huntington Library, but with the additions found in other copies as read also by Cobo.

33. Herrera derived his reference to the forty wives of Atahuallpa from the *Relación* describing the festivities, from 20 to 28 February 1631, celebrating the birth of the prince Don Baltasar Carlos in Madrid a year and a half earlier. The festivities included a representation of the Inca king and his forty wives. The *Relación* is found in volume 95, folios 88r–92v, Archivo Municipal, Quito.

34. Most important in Pizarro's information, used also by Cobo (Bk. 12, Ch. 36), are the details about the hierarchy of the "sisters" and concubines and the rotation of their presence with the king. The detail of the 41 weeks of 8 days still leaves many questions unanswered; one of them pertains to the agricultural calendar and is of a more technical nature. What happened during the remaining 37-day period of the year not accounted for? A rotation

similar to that of the "sisters" of the king is mentioned by Garcilaso (Bk. 3, Ch. 22; Bk. 6, Ch. 35) for the priests in the Temple of the Sun. The imperial court in ancient China also knew a rotation of wives of the emperor according to a lunar calendar (see, e.g., Needham, Ling and de Solla Price 1960 p. 171).

35. For a discussion and reconstruction of this calendar, see Zuidema 1982b; 1982c; 1985b; 1986; 1988; 1989b; 1989c; 1989d; in press a; in press d.

The Inca calendar, in its concern with agricultural activities from plowing and planting to harvest, only counted a period of 328 days in the year. Such a period is equal to that of twelve sidereal months of 27⅓ days each, resulting from a type of lunar observation that takes into account, rather than the moon's phases, its various positions in relation to the stars. The period of 328 days is also equal to 41 "weeks" of 8 days. For the special interest that the Incas had in the remaining period of 37 days, devoted to their relations with other non-Inca lords, see Zuidema in press c.

36. Molina "el Cuzqueño" 1943 p. 28; Cobo Bk. 13, Ch. 28. Although the Tarpuntay formed one of the ten non-noble *ayllus,* according to José de Acosta (Bk. 5, Ch. 22), they were the descendants of the priest-king Lloque Yupanqui (no. 3) from Hurin-Cuzco. This information gives us to understand that Murúa (Bk. 1, Ch. 7) also refers to the same period of fasting when discussing this king.

37. Especially the text of Sarmiento (Ch. 47) makes clear that Hatun Ayllu and Iñaca Panaca are two names for one and the same group, and that they do not indicate two different groups as is claimed by Rostworowski (1983 p. 143). See also Zuidema 1989c.

38. For a similar use of the *iñaca* title elsewhere, see Taylor Ch. 39, p. 347, and Rowe 1966 p. 38.

39. See also Zuidema 1989a, where I develop further the theme of the double role in marriage of these ladies: as principal wife of a local lord and, at the same time, as concubine of the king to whom they gave the children that he called *concha,* "nephew" or "niece." See also Espinoza Soriano (1976).

40. See Barraud et al. 1984, who analyze such a concept of exchange, operating as it does in various cultures.

41. E.g., Bauer 1987; Niles 1987.

42. E.g., Molinié Fioravanti 1982; Poole 1984; Urton 1984; 1986; 1988; 1990.

43. See also Conrad and Demarest 1984 and a critique of their position on this point by W. Isbell (1981).

Glossary

aclla: chosen woman
ayllu: a social unit and/or kin group
caca: mother's brother; wife's brother or father
cacacuna: male relatives of the wife and the mother
cacacuzco: original, pre-Inca inhabitants of the Cuzco Valley
capac: royal
ceque: sightline
chapa: district
concha: child of a man's sister, secondary child
curaca: lord
huaca: sacred place
huaccha: orphan, poor
iñaca: non-Inca noble woman
ipa: father's sister
mita: labor taken in turns
mitima: person who has been relocated temporarily or permanently
mulla: child of a woman's brother
pana: sister of a man
panaca: descendants of a *concha*
sullca: youngest (fourth) child
suyu: one of the four provinces of the Inca Empire
Tarpuntay: "planter," priest of the sun
"Visitas": administrative inspections

◄ Bibliography ►

Abbreviations used

AA: American Antiquity.
AAA: American Anthropological Association.
BAE: Biblioteca de Autores Españoles. Madrid: Atlas.
IEP: Instituto de Estudios Peruanos.
IFEA: Instituto Francés de Estudios Andinos. Lima.
JLAL: Journal of Latin American Lore. Los Angeles.
JSA: Journal de la Société des Américanistes. Paris.
JSAS: Journal of the Steward Anthropological Society. Urbana, Ill.
RA: Revista Andina.
REAA: Revista Española de Antropología Americana. Madrid.
RI: Revista de Indias.
RMN: Revista del Museo Nacional. Lima.

Abercrombie, Thomas A. 1986. The Politics of Sacrifice: An Aymara Cosmology in Action. Ph.D. dissertation, University of Chicago.

Acosta, Antonio. 1987. Estudio biográfico sobre Francisco de Avila. In Taylor 1987:551–616.

Acosta, José de. 1954. *Historia natural y moral de las Indias* (1590). BAE 73.

Alberti Manzanares, Pilar. 1985. La influencia económica y política de las acllacuna en el Incanato. *RI* 45(176): 557–585.

———. 1986. Una institución exclusivamente femenina en la época incaica: Las acllacuna. *REAA* 16:151–190.

———. 1987. Mujer y religión: Vestales y acllacuna, dos instituciones religiosas de mujeres. *REAA* 17.

Arguedas, José María. 1956. Puquio, una cultura en proceso de cambio. *RMN* 25.

————, trans. 1966. *Dioses y hombres de Huarochirí: Narración quechua recogida por Francisco de Avila* (1598?). Lima: Museo Nacional de Historia/IEP.

Arriaga, Pablo José de. 1968. *Extirpación de la idolatría del Perú* (1621). BAE 219.

Avila, Francisco de. *See* A. Acosta 1987; Arguedas, trans. 1966; Duviols 1966; Salomon n.d.

Bandera, Damián de la. 1881. *Relación general de la disposición y calidad de la Provincia de Guamanga* (1557). Relaciones Geográficas de Indias 1 : 98–103. Also in BAE 183 : 176–180 (1965).

Barraud, Cécile, Daniel de Coppet, André Iteanu, and Raymond Jamous. 1984. Des relations et des morts: Quatre sociétés vues sous l'angle des échanges. In *Différences, valeurs, hiérarchie: Textes offerts à Louis Dumont*, edited by Jean-Claude Galey, pp. 421–520. Paris: Editions de l'Ecole des Hautes Etudes en Sciences Sociales.

Bataillon, Marcel. 1960. Un chroniqueur péruvien retrouvé: RODRIGO LOZANO. *Cahiers de l'Institut des Hautes Etudes de l'Amérique Latine* 1960 : 5–25.

————. 1961. Gutiérrez de Santa Clara, escritor mexicano. *Nueva Revista de Filología Hispánica* 15 : 3–4.

————. 1963–1964. Zárate ou Lozano? Pages retrouvées sur la religion péruvienne. *Caravelle: Cahiers du Monde Hispanique et Luso-Brésilien* 1–3 : 11–28.

Bauer, Brian S. 1987. Sistemas andinos de organización rural antes del establecimiento de reducciones: El ejemplo de Pacariqtambo, Perú. *RA* 5(1) : 197–210.

Bertonio, Ludovico. 1956. *Vocabulario de la lengua Aymara* (1612). La Paz.

Betanzos, Juan de. 1968. *Suma y narración de los Incas* (1551). BAE 219.

————. 1987. *Suma y narración de los Incas* (1551), edited by María del Carmen Martín Rubio. Madrid: Atlas.

Bidou, Patrice. 1976. Les fils de l'Anaconda céleste (les Tatuyo): Etude de la structure socio-politique. Ph.D. thesis, University of Paris.

Bolton, Ralph, and Enrique Mayer, eds. 1977. *Andean Kinship and Marriage*. Washington, D.C.: AAA Special Publication No. 7. (*See also* the Spanish edition, Mayer and Bolton, eds. 1980.)

Calancha, Antonio de la. 1981. *Crónica moralizada* (1638). Transcription, critical study, bibliographic notes, and indices by Ignacio Prado Pastor. Lima: Prado Pastor.

Castro, Cristóbal de, and Diego de Ortega y Morejón. *See* Trimborn, ed. 1936.

Cereceda, Verónica. 1987. Aproximaciones a una estética andina: De la belleza al *tinku*. In *Tres reflexiones sobre el pensamiento andino*, pp. 133–231. La Paz: Hisbol.

Cieza de León, Pedro de. 1945. *La crónica del Perú* (1551). Buenos Aires.

——. 1967. *El señorío de los Incas* (1551). Lima.

Cobo, Bernabé. 1956. *Historia del nuevo mundo* (1653), vol. 2. BAE.

——. *History of the Inca Empire*. Translated by Roland Hamilton. Austin: University of Texas Press, 1979. (Translation of Books 11–12 of *Historia del nuevo mundo*.)

Collapiña, Supno, and other Quipucamayos. 1974. *Relación de la descendencia, gobierno y conquista de los Incas*. Prologue by Juan José Vega. Lima: Biblioteca Universitaria.

Conrad, G. W. 1981. Cultural Materialism, Split Inheritance, and the Expansion of Ancient Peruvian Empires. *AA* 46:38–42.

Conrad, G. W., and Arthur A. Demarest. 1984. *Religion and Empire: The Dynamics of Aztec and Inca Expansionism*. Cambridge: Cambridge University Press.

Cook, D. N. 1981. *Demographic Collapse: Indian Peru, 1520–1620*. Cambridge: Cambridge University Press.

Dumézil, Georges. 1973. Mater Matuta. In *Mythe et epopée: Histoires romaines*, pp. 305–330. Paris: Gallimard.

Duviols, Pierre. 1964. La historia del descubrimiento y de la conquista del Perú de Agustin de Zárate remaniée conformément aux vues historico-politiques du Vice-Roi Toledo. *Annales de la Faculté des Lettres d'Aix* 38:151–155.

——. 1966. Estudio biobibliográfico: Francisco de Avila, extirpador de la idolatría. In Arguedas, trans. 1966:218–266.

——. 1971. *La Lutte contre les religions autochtones dans le Pérou colonial: "L'Extirpation de l'idolâtrie entre 1532 et 1660."* Lima: IFEA.

——. 1974–1976. Une petite chronique retrouvée: Errores, ritos, supersticiones y ceremonias de los yndios . . . de Chinchaycocha. *JSA* 63.

——. 1979. La dinastía de los Incas: ¿Monarquía o diarquía? Argumentos heurísticos a favor de una tesis estructuralista. *JSA* 64:67–83.

——. 1986. *Cultura andina y represión: Procesos y visitas de idolatrías y hechicerías, Cajatambo, Siglo XVII*. Archivos de Historia Andina, vol. 5. Cuzco: Centro de Estudios Rurales Andinos "Bartolomé de las Casas."

Earls, John. 1971. The Structure of Modern Andean Social Categories. *JSAS* 3(1).

Espinoza Soriano, Waldemar. 1976. Las mujeres secundarias de Huayna Capac: Dos casos de señorialismo feudal en el Imperio Inca. *RMN* 42:247–298.

Garcilaso de la Vega, El Inca. 1966. *Royal Commentaries of the Incas* (1609), Part One. Translated by Harold V. Livermore. Austin: University of Texas Press.

González Holguín, Diego. 1952. *Vocabulario de la lengua . . . Qquichua* (1608). Lima.

Guaman Poma de Ayala, Felipe. 1986. *El primer neuva crónica y buen gobierno* (1583–1615). Edited by John V. Murra, Rolena Adorno, and Jorge L. Urioste. Madrid: Historia 16.

Gutiérrez de Santa Clara, Pedro. 1963–1964. *Historia de las guerras civiles del Perú . . .* (1600?). BAE 165–167.

Héritier, Françoise. 1981. *L'Exercice de la parenté*. Paris: Gallimard Le Seuil.

Herrera, Pablo. 1916. *Apunte cronológico de las obras y trabajos del cabildo y municipalidad de Quito desde 1534 hasta 1714 (primera época)*, vol. 1. Quito.

Hernández Príncipe, Rodrigo. 1986. Visitas to Ocros, Sta María Magdalena and Recuay (1621–1622). In Duviols 1986:461–507.

Hugh-Jones, Christine. 1979. *From the Milk River: Spatial and Temporal Processes in Northwest Amazonia*. Cambridge: Cambridge University Press.

Hugh-Jones, Stephen. 1979. *The Palm and the Pleiades: Initiation and Cosmology in Northwest Amazonia*. Cambridge: Cambridge University Press.

Imbelloni, José. 1946. *Pachakuti IX (El Inkario Crítico)*. Buenos Aires: Editorial Humanior.

Isbell, Billie Jean. 1977. "Those Who Love Me": An Analysis of Andean Kinship and Reciprocity within a Ritual Context. In Bolton and Mayer, eds. 1977:81–105.

———. 1978. *To Defend Ourselves: Ecology and Ritual in an Andean Village*. Austin: University of Texas Press.

———. 1983. The Ethnographic Context for Acquiring and Transforming Andean Culture. Unpublished paper.

Isbell, William. 1981. Comment on Conrad. *American Antiquity* 46:27–30.

Las Casas, Bartolomé de. 1958. *Apologética Historia* (1564). BAE 106.

Le Roy Ladurie, Emmanuel. 1973. Système de la Cour (Versailles, vers 1709). In *Le Territoire de l'historien* 2:275–299. Paris: Gallimard.

Lounsbury, Floyd G. 1964. Some Aspects of the Inca Kinship System. Paper presented at the 36th International Congress of Americanists, Barcelona.

Mannheim, Bruce. 1986. The Language of Reciprocity in Southern Peruvian Quechua. *Anthropological Linguistics*, Fall 1986, pp. 267–273.

Martyr Coma, Pedro. 1574. *Libro intitulado directorium curatorum*. Zaragoza: Miguel de Guessa.

Masuda, Shozo, Izumi Shimada, and Craig Morris, eds. 1985. *Andean Ecology and Civilization: An Interdisciplinary Perspective on Andean Ecological Complementarity*. Tokyo: University of Tokyo Press.

Maybury-Lewis, David. 1967. *Akwe-Shavante Society*. Oxford: Clarendon Press.

Mayer, Enrique, and Ralph Bolton, eds. 1980. *Parentesco y matrimonio en los Andes*. Lima: Pontificia Universidad Católica del Perú.

Molina "el Almagrista," Cristóbal de. 1968. *Relación de muchas cosas acaecidas en el Perú* . . . (1553). In *Crónicas peruanas de interés indígena*, edited by F. Esteve Barba, pp. 57–95. BAE 209. (According to Rowe, the writer is Bartolomé de Segovia.)

Molina "el Cuzqueño," Cristóbal de. 1925. Información hecha en el Cuzco . . . acerca de las costumbres que tenían los Incas del Perú . . . Declaran García de Melo, Damián de la Bandera, el rev. P. Cristóbal de Molina, Alonso de Mesa, Bartolomé de Porras y algunos Indios (1582). In *Gobernantes del Perú*, by Roberto Leviller, 9:268–296. Madrid: Imprenta de Juan Pueyo.

———. 1943. *Fábulas y ritos de los Incas* (1573). Lima.

Molinié Fioravanti, Antoinette. 1982. *La Vallée sacrée des Andes*. Recherches Américaines 4. Paris: Société d' Ethnographie.

Murra, John V. 1975. *Formaciones económicas y políticas del mundo andino*. Lima: IEP.

———. 1980. *The Economic Organization of the Inka State*. Greenwich, Conn.: JAI Press Inc. (Publication of Ph.D. dissertation, 1956.)

Murúa, Martín. 1962. *Historia general del Perú* . . . (1611–1618). Madrid.

Needham, Joseph, Wang Ling, and Derek J. de Solla Price. 1960. *Heavenly Clockwork: The Great Astronomical Clocks of Medieval China*. Cambridge: Cambridge University Press.

Niles, Susan A. 1987. *Callachaca: Style and Status in an Inca Community*. Iowa City: University of Iowa Press.

Nimuendajú, Curt. 1946. *The Eastern Timbira*. Berkeley: University of California Press.

Ossio, Juan M. 1980. La estructura social de las comunidades andinas. In *Historia del Perú*, edited by Juan Mejía Baca, 3:205–377. Lima: Mejía Baca.

———. 1983. El estudio de la estructura social en las comunidades andinas. In *La cuestión rural en el Perú*, edited by Javier Iguiñiz, pp. 165–194. Lima: Pontificia Universidad Católica del Perú.

———. 1984. Cultural Continuity, Structure, and Context: Some Peculiarities of the Andean *Compadrazgo*. In *Kinship Ideology and Practice in Latin America*, edited by Raymond T. Smith, pp. 118–146. Chapel Hill: University of North Carolina Press.

Pérez Bocanegra, Juan. 1631. *Ritual formulario* . . . Lima.

Pizarro, Pedro. 1978. *Relación del descubrimiento y conquista de los reinos del Perú* (1571). Edited and with preliminary considerations by G. Lohmann

Villena, and with a note by Pierre Duviols. Lima: Pontificia Universidad Católica del Perú.

Poole, Deborah A. 1984. Ritual-Economic Calendars in Paruro: The Structures of Representation in Andean Ethnography. Ph.D. dissertation, Department of Anthropology, University of Illinois, Urbana.

Relación de las costumbres antiguas de los naturales del Pirú (ca. 1590). 1950. Reproduction of the edition by Marcos Jiménez de la Espada. In *Tres relaciones de antigüedades peruanas*. (Author sometimes given as Blas Valera.) Asunción del Paraguay: Editorial Guaranía.

Ricardo, Antonio (original ed.). 1951. *Vocabulario . . . Quichua* (1586). Lima.

Rostworowski de Diez Canseco, María. 1962. Nuevos datos sobre tenencia de tierras reales en el Incario. *RMN* 31.

———. 1970. Mercaderes del valle de Chincha . . . *REAA* 5.

———. 1983. *Estructuras andinas del poder: Ideología religiosa y política*. Lima: IEP.

———. 1988. *Historia del Tahuantinsuyu*. Lima: IEP.

Rowe, John Howland. 1946. Inca Culture at the Time of the Spanish Conquest. In *Handbook of South American Indians* 2 : 183–330. Washington, D.C.: Bureau of American Ethnology Bulletin 143.

———. 1958. The Age Grades of the Inca Census. In *Miscellanea Paul Rivet*. XXXIst Congress of Americanists, Mexico.

———. 1966. Un memorial del gobierno de los Incas del año 1551. *Revista Peruana de Cultura* 9–10 : 27–39.

———. 1967. What Kind of Settlement Was Inca Cuzco? *Ñawpa Pacha* 5 : 59–76.

———. 1979. An Account of the Shrines of Ancient Cuzco. *Ñawpa Pacha* 17 : 2–80.

———. 1985. La constitución Inca del Cuzco. *Histórica* 9(1).

Salomon, Frank. n.d. The Huarochiri Manuscript: A Testament of Ancient and Colonial Andean Religion. Introductory Essay. Unpublished.

Santacruz Pachacuti Yamqui Salcamaygua, Joan de. 1950. *Relación de antigüedades deste reyno del Pirú* (1613). Reproduction of the edition by Marcos Jiménez de la Espada. In *Tres relaciones de antigüedades peruanas*. Asunción del Paraguay: Editorial Guaranía.

Santillán, Fernando de. 1950. *Relación del origen, descendencia, política y gobierno de los Incas* (1563). Reproduction of the edition by Marcos Jiménez de la Espada. In *Tres relaciones de antigüedades peruanas*. Asunción del Paraguay: Editorial Guaranía.

Santo Tomás, Domingo de. 1951. *Lexicón . . . de la lengua general del Perú* (1560). Lima.

Sarmiento de Gamboa, Pedro. 1947. *Historia de los Incas* (1572). Buenos Aires: Emecé.

Sherbondy, Jeanette E. 1979. Les Réseaux d'irrigation dans la géographie politique de Cuzco. *JSA* 66:45–66.

———. 1982a. The Canal System of Hanan Cuzco. Ph.D. dissertation, Department of Anthropology, University of Illinois, Urbana.

———. 1982b. El regadío, los lagos y los mitos de origen. *Allpanchis* 17(20):3–32.

———. 1986. Los *ceques:* Código de canales en el Cuzco Incaico. *Allpanchis,* no. 27:39–74.

———. 1987. Organización hidráulica y poder en el Cuzco de los Incas. *REAA* 17:117–154.

Taylor, Gerald. 1987. *Ritos y tradiciones de Huarochiri del siglo XVII.* Lima: IEP/IFEA.

Trimborn, Hermann, ed. 1936. "Relación y declaración del modo que este valle de Chincha y sus comarcanos se governavan Antes que oviese Yngas y despues q(ue) los vuo hast q(ue) los (christian)os e(n)traron en esta tierra," by Cristóbal de Castro and Diego de Ortega y Morejón. In *Quellen zur Kulturgeschichte des präkolumbischen Amerika,* pp. 236–246. Stuttgart.

Urbano, Henrique Osvaldo. 1981. *Wiracocha y Ayar: Héroes y funciones en las sociedades andinas.* Biblioteca de la Tradición Oral Andina no. 3. Cuzco: Centro de Estudios Rurales Andinos "Bartolomé de las Casas."

Urton, Gary. 1984. Ch'uta: El espacio de la práctica social en Pacariqtambo, Perú. *RA* 2(1):7–56.

———. 1986. Calendrical Cycles and Their Projections in Pacariqtambo, Peru. *JLAL* 12(1):45–64.

———. 1988. La arquitectura pública como texto social: La historia de un muro de adobe in Pacariqtambo, Perú (1915–1985). *RA* 6(1):225–261.

———. 1990. *The History of a Myth: Pacariqtambo and the Origin of the Inkas.* Austin: University of Texas Press.

Villanueva Urteaga, Horacio, and Jeanette Sherbondy. 1984. *Cuzco: Aguas y poder.* Centro de Estudios Rurales Andinos "Bartolomé de las Casas."

Wachtel, Nathan. 1971. *La Vision des vaincus: Les Indiens du Pérou devant la conquête espagnole.* Paris: Gallimard.

———. 1973. *Sociedad e ideología: Ensayos de historia y antropología andinas.* Lima: IEP.

———. 1980–1981. Les Mitimaes de la vallée de Cochabamba . . . *JSA* 67.

Zárate, Agustín de. 1555. *Historia del Perú.* Antwerp.

———. 1968. *The Discovery and Conquest of Peru.* Translated with an introduction by J. M. Cohen. Baltimore: Penguin Books.

Zuidema, R. Tom. 1964. *The Ceque System of Cuzco: The Social Organization of the Capital of the Inca*. Leiden: E. J. Brill.

———. 1973a. Kinship and Ancestor Cult in Three Peruvian Communities: Hernández Príncipe's Account in 1622. *Boletín del IFEA* 2(10):16–33.

———. 1973b. La Quadrature du cercle dans l'ancien Pérou. *Signes et Langages des Amériques: Recherches Amérindiennes au Québec* 3(1/2):147–165.

———. 1977a. The Inca Kinship System: A New Theoretical View. In Bolton and Mayer, eds. 1977:240–281.

———. 1977b. The Inca Calendar. In *Native American Astronomy*, edited by Anthony F. Aveni, pp. 219–259. Austin: University of Texas Press.

———. 1977–1978. Shafttombs and the Inca Empire. *JSAS* 9(1/2).

———. 1981. Inca Observations of the Solar and Lunar Passages through Zenith and Anti-Zenith at Cuzco. In *Archaeoastronomy in the Americas*, edited by Ray A. Williamson, pp. 319–342. Los Altos: Ballena Press.

———. 1982a. Myth and History in Ancient Peru. In *The Logic of Culture*, edited by I. Rossi, pp. 150–175. South Hadley, Mass.: Bergin.

———. 1982b. Catachillay, the Role of the Pleiades and of the Southern Cross and α and β Centauri in the Calendar of the Incas. In *Ethnoastronomy and Archaeoastronomy in the American Tropics*, edited by Anthony F. Aveni and Gary Urton, pp. 203–229. Annals of the New York Academy of Sciences 385. New York.

———. 1982c. The Sidereal-Lunar Calendar of the Incas. In *New World Archaeoastronomy*, edited by Anthony F. Aveni. Cambridge: Cambridge University Press.

———. 1983. Hierarchy and Space in Incaic Social Organization. *Ethnohistory* 30(2):49–75.

———. 1985a. The Lion in the City. In *Animal Myths and Metaphors*, edited by Gary Urton, pp. 183–250. Salt Lake City: University of Utah Press. (Republication of *JLAL* 9[1]:39–100 [1983].)

———. 1985b. L'Organisation andine du savoir rituel et technique en termes d'espace et du temps. *Techniques et Cultures* 6:43–66.

———. 1986. Inka Dynasty and Irrigation: Another Look at Andean Concepts of History. In *Anthropological History of Andean Polities*, edited by J. V. Murra, N. Wachtel, and J. Revel, pp. 177–200. Cambridge: Cambridge University Press/Editions de la Maison des Sciences de l'Homme. (Republication of *Annales* 33[5/6]:1037–1056 [1978].)

———. 1988. The Pillars of Cuzco: Which Two Dates of Sunset Did They Define? In *New Directions in American Archaeoastronomy*, edited by Anthony F. Aveni, pp. 143–169. Oxford: BAR International Series 454.

———. 1989a. What Does the Equation "Mother's Brother = Wife's Father"

Mean in Inca Social Organization? In *Variant Views: Five Lectures from the Perspective of the "Leiden Tradition" in Cultural Anthropology,* edited by H. J. M. Claessen, pp. 132–156. Leiden: Universiteit van Leiden, Faculteit der Sociale Wetenschappen, Vakgroep Culturele Anthropologie en Sociologie der Niet-Westerse Samenlevingen (ICA Publicatie: no. 84).

———. 1989b. A Quipu Calendar from Ica, Peru, with a Comparison to the Ceque Calendar from Cuzco. In *World Archaeoastronomy: Selected Papers from the 2nd Oxford International Conference on Archaeoastronomy Held at Merida, Yucatan, Mexico, 13–17 January 1986,* edited by Anthony F. Aveni, pp. 341–351. Cambridge: Cambridge University Press.

———. 1989c. The Moieties of Cuzco. In *The Attraction of Opposites: Thought and Society in the Dualistic Mode,* edited by David Maybury-Lewis and Uri Amagor. Ann Arbor: University of Michigan Press.

———. 1989d. At The King's Table: Inca Concepts of Sacred Kingship in Cuzco. *History and Anthropology* 4:249–274.

———. 1990. *Reyes y guerreros.* Lima: Fomciencias. (This volume contains the Spanish translations of Zuidema 1973a, 1973b, 1977a, 1977–1978, 1982a, and 1985a.)

———. In press a. Ceques and Chapas: An Andean Pattern of Land Partition in the Modern Valley of Cuzco. In *Papers in Honor of Professor Th. S. Bartel.*

———. In press b. Dynastic Structures in Andean Culture. In *Kingship and Statecraft in Chimor,* edited by M. Moseley and M. Rostworowsky. Washington, D.C.: Dumbarton Oaks.

———. In press c. Lllama Sacrifices and Computation: Roots of the Inca Calendar in Huari-Tiahuanaco Culture. *Acts of the Congress on Ethnoastronomy, Held in Washington, D.C., 1983.*

———. In press d. The Technical Use of Ceques in Andean Culture. In *La tecnología en el mundo andino,* vol. 2, edited by H. Lechtman and A. M. Soldi. Mexico City: Universidad Nacional Autónoma de México.

Zuidema, R. Tom, and Deborah A. Poole. 1982. Los límites de los cuatro suyus incaicos en el Cuzco. *Boletín del IFEA* 9(1/2):83–89.

Zuidema, R. Tom, and Gary Urton. 1976. La constelación de la Llama en los Andes peruanos. *Allpanchis Phuturinqa* 9:59–119.